Lernkrimi Englisch

Last Exit Waterloo Bridge

Bernie Martin
Sarah Trenker

compact

Weitere Informationen zu Compact Lernkrimis finden Sie am Ende des Buches und unter www.lernkrimi.de.

Baierbrunner Str. 27, 81379 München
Ausgabe 2015
10. Auflage

Chefredaktion: Dr. Matthias Feldbaum
Redaktion: Helga Aichele
Fachkorrektur: Alison Frankland
Produktion: Ute Hausleiter
Titelillustration: Karl Knospe
Lernkrimi-Logo: Carsten Abelbeck
Gestaltung: Maria Seidel
Umschlaggestaltung: EKH Werbeagentur GbR, Hartmut Baier

ISBN 978-3-8174-7733-3
7277334/10

www.compactverlag.de, www.lernkrimi.de

Vorwort

Mit den neuen, spannenden Compact Kurzkrimis können Sie Ihre Englischkenntnisse auf schnelle und einfache Weise vertiefen, auffrischen und überprüfen.
Die vier fesselnden Kurzkrimis sind ideal für geübte Anfänger und Wiedereinsteiger.
Jeder Krimi wird durch abwechslungsreiche und kurzweilige Übungen ergänzt, die das Lernen unterhaltsam und spannend machen. Prüfen Sie Ihr Englisch in Lückentexten, Zuordnungs- und Übersetzungsaufgaben, in Buchstabenspielen und Kreuzworträtseln!
Ob im Bus oder in der Bahn, im Wartezimmer, zu Hause oder in der Mittagspause – das Sprachtraining im handlichen Format bietet die ideale Trainingsmöglichkeit für zwischendurch.
Schreiben Sie die Lösungen einfach ins Buch!
Die richtigen Antworten sind in einem eigenen Lösungsteil am Ende des Buches zusammengefasst. Im Anhang befindet sich außerdem ein Glossar, in dem die schwierigsten Wörter übersetzt sind. Diese sind im Text kursiv markiert.

Und nun kann die Spannung beginnen ...

Viel Spaß und Erfolg!

Inhalt

Terminus Waterloo Bridge
Ein Profikiller kommt nach London, um den Tod seiner Familie zu rächen. Aber auf wen genau hat er es abgesehen? Und kann Inspector Roberta Fletcher ihn rechtzeitig aufhalten?

A Nice Neighbourhood
In einem kleinen Dorf in East Anglia sind kurz hintereinander drei Männer gestorben. Alle drei waren Zugezogene und nicht sehr beliebt im Dorf. Doch war es Mord? Wer hatte ein Motiv?

Murder in Battersea Park
Beim Joggen im Londoner Battersea Park entdeckt ein junger Wachtmeister eine Tote auf der Parkbank. Warum wurde sie ermordet? Die Befragungen im Bekanntenkreis der Toten beginnen ...

Catching a Big Fish
Ein herrenloses Boot am Strand von Shelterwind Cove gibt Detective Ramsey Rätsel auf – gibt es eine Verbindung zu der Entführung des Millionärs James Churchill? Kann das Boot die Polizei auf die Spur der Entführer bringen?

TERMINUS WATERLOO BRIDGE

Bernie Martin

Chapter 1: The Killer

Nobody knows his real name. The professional killer known as "Marco" sits in a jet on his way from Rome to London and thinks about his mission. He spent the last few years getting *revenge* on the people who killed his family. Now there is only one person left on his list and that person is in London.

Marco closes his eyes and falls into a troubled sleep.

Once again he sees himself as a small boy: he is getting water for his family from the *stream*. Then he hears the *scream* of the *rockets* that are flying over his head, racing towards his village. The sound of the *rockets* is still very clear to him and he jumps in his sleep. His *body jerks* in his seat as he *relives* the explosions and the terrible *screams* of the *villagers*. He runs to his home in shock, *whispering* thc name of his parents and his little sister, Jasmin. The first thing he notices is the smell of burnt flesh, the flesh of people, then he sees what is left of his home. The hot, bitter tears come and he runs to the living area of his home. He sees his father first. The old Enfield *rifle* is still warm in his father's hand. He shot at the jets. Marco shakes his head at his father's courage. Marco closes his father's eyes and lets out a great *scream* of pain. His *scream* is suddenly cut off when he sees his mother's sandal sticking out of the *remains* of their house. He *crawls* across the stones and sees that his mother died because she was trying to protect her daughter, Jasmin. Marco *gently* rolls his mother's *body* off his sister, lifts her in his arms and carries her to the foot of a tree where there is shade.

Jasmin moans "water" and Marco looks around for the water bucket.

It is only twenty yards away, but Marco can't remember carrying it that far. He jumps up and collects the bucket as fast as he can. He places the bucket next to Jasmin and bends down to lift her head so that she can drink.
"Marco. I'm cold."
Marco panics because it is a very hot day.
"It's okay, Jasmin. I'm here."
"Marco. Why is it getting dark so early? I don't understand."
Jasmin *squeezes* Marco's hand, gives one last sigh and dies in his arms.
"Jasmin! Don't go! You can't leave me alone. Come back, Jasmin. Please, come back."
Tears stream down Marco's face. He lays his sister down with great care, not wanting to hurt her. He cries a few *prayers* for her *soul* and then stands up. He angrily shakes his fist at the sky and screams: "I will have my *revenge*!"

ÜBUNG 1

Übung 1: Welche Übersetzung stimmt? Kreuzen Sie an!

1. Marco, mir ist kalt.
   a) ☐ Marco. I am cold.
   b) ☐ Marco. I am a cold person.

2. Er sieht seinen Vater zuerst.
   a) ☐ His father sees him first.
   b) ☐ He sees his father first.

3. Marco schüttelt seinen Kopf.
   a) ☐ Marco shakes his head.
   b) ☐ Marco nods his head.

4. Ich verstehe nicht.
   a) ☐ I understand not.
   b) ☐ I don't understand.

5. Du kannst mich nicht alleine lassen.
   a) ☐ You should leave me alone.
   b) ☐ You can't leave me alone.

"Would you like something to drink before we land, sir?"
Marco wakes up to see a pretty stewardess smile at him.
"No thank you. I'm fine."
"We'll land at Heathrow in about ten minutes, sir. Could you please fasten your seat belt?"
Marco smiles, *nods* and fastens his seat belt. He is still sweating from his dream. His last thought before he lands is: "When this last person is dead and my family is revenged, maybe then I can dream the dreams of a child again."

Thirty minutes later, Ali is waiting for Marco in the arrivals area. He will meet Marco for the first time. He only knows the legend. Marco is his hero. He looks for a man in a beige suit, with a black *carnation* pinned to the jacket. This is the agreed *recognition signal* and Ali is very excited. Then he sees him and his heart misses a beat. Marco is a slim, handsome man with short black hair. Ali *waves* and the man smiles, showing very white teeth. As Marco *approaches*, Ali sees that his eyes are completely black. A little *shiver* of fear goes through Ali when he realizes that the smile on the mouth is in complete contrast to the *deadliness* of the eyes. He *grabs* Marco's hands.
"Greetings, Master!"
"Hello, Ali. You weren't followed, were you?"

"No, Master. I have the car waiting. I will drive you to the *safe house*."

Marco *nods*. "The *arms dealer*?"

"He is expecting you, master. Should I drive you there now?"

"No. Tomorrow will be soon enough."

ÜBUNG 2 !

Übung 2: Welches Wort ist das „schwarze Schaf"? Unterstreichen Sie das nicht in die Reihe passende Wort!

1. see, sea, saw, seen
2. smile, grin, cry, laugh
3. jacket, trousers, coat, anorak
4. boys, childs, girls, children
5. eyes, feet, nose, mouth
6. handsome, slim, beautiful, pretty
7. car, lorry, truck, motorbike

The next day, Ali drives Marco to the *arms dealer* in Soho. Marco tells Ali to wait in the car with the *engine* running.

Marco enters the *newsagent's* shop and locks the door behind him. There is a fat man behind the *counter*. He has dark, *greasy* hair and is very nervous. He looks at Marco with fear in his eyes and says, "Good morning. Can I help you?"

"It is very cold in London today."

The fat man recognizes the code.

"You want to buy weapons?"

"Yes."

"Follow me."

The fat man goes to a room at the back of the shop. He pushes a table and carpet aside. There is a door in the floor and he lifts it.

Marco sees steps to the cellar and he follows the fat man down. The room is full of weapons. Marco picks up a gun and looks at it. He can see that the fat man is still afraid.

"Why are you so nervous?"

"Just tell me what you want and leave."

"You aren't very polite, Mr...?"

"No names. Now, what do you want to buy?"

Marco chooses some weapons and asks the fat man the price.

"Ten thousand pounds."

"Too expensive. I'll give you five thousand."

"I have to live, you know. I'll take seven thousand and give you ten boxes of *ammunition*."

Marco agrees and pays cash. The fat man's hands shake as he packs the guns in brown paper. Marco takes the packages and goes up the stairs. He walks to the shop door and unlocks it. He opens the door and Ali gets out of the car. Marco gives him the packages and *whispers*, "Drive round the block."

Ali *nods*. Marco goes back into the shop, closes the door and hides behind some *bookshelves*. A few minutes later he hears the fat man close the door to the cellar. The fat man then hurries to the shop door, nervously looks out and locks the door. Then he goes to the phone on the *counter* and *dials* a number.

"Hello. Is that the police?"

"Yes, sir. How can I help you?"

"Shut up and listen. I want to speak to Inspector Fletcher. We have a deal."

"Could you give me your name, please?"

"Tell Fletcher that Adam Giles phoned. She promised I wouldn't go to prison. Someone just bought two *rifles* and two handguns from me."

Marco quietly moves towards the *counter*.

"Mr Giles, could you give me your address, sir?"
"Yes. It's... Aargh!"

ÜBUNG 3 !

Übung 3: Übersetzen Sie die folgenden Aussagen!

1. Ich möchte Inspector Fletcher sprechen.

____

2. Sie sind nicht sehr höflich.

____

3. Guten Morgen, kann ich Ihnen helfen?

____

4. Warum sind Sie so nervös?

____

5. Ali steigt aus dem Auto aus.

____

6. Er geht zur Ladentür und schließt sie auf.

____

Marco doesn't want anyone to hear the sound of a gun, so he pulls the *piano wire* tight around the fat man's neck. He lowers the *body* to the floor behind the *counter*. He quickly looks out of the window to check if people on the busy street have noticed anything. But the *pedestrians* just walk on. Good. Marco goes to the door and *waves* to Ali at the end of the street. Marco jumps in the car and they drive off.

The telephone is still swinging in the air. A voice can be heard.
"Mr Giles! Are you still there? Is something wrong?"

Chapter 2: Fletcher and Walsh

A short time later, Inspector Roberta Fletcher of the Metropolitan Police is sitting at her desk. There is a knock at the door.
"Come in."
Roberta's assistant Jack Walsh enters the room. Roberta looks at him and sees a very fit man in his thirties, who goes to a fitness club every day of the year. He has bright red hair and wears glasses with thick black frames. Jack is a *confirmed bachelor*. He still lives with his mother in Wembley. His passion is researching murder *cases* from the nineteenth century.
Roberta smiles at his *tweed* suit and colourful *dickie bow*.
"Jack, I'll have to take you shopping for clothes. You look like a very boring English professor."
Jack *stares* into her brown eyes.
"Yes, Roberta. You say that at least once a week."
Jack is interrupted by Roberta's telephone. She picks it up.
"Inspector Fletcher here?"
"Hello, Inspector. This is *Constable* Foster. I *received* a call from a Mr Adam Giles a few minutes ago. He asked for you by name."
"I know Mr Giles, *Constable*. What does he want?"
"Well, that's the strange thing, Inspector. He seemed to be cut off, but I could hear *choking noises* in the background."
Roberta starts taking notes. "Did he give you his address?"
"No, but I have it here on my computer screen."
"Okay. Give it to me please."
"It's Adam Giles, 38 Frith Street, a *newsagent's* in Soho."

"Right, thanks. We're on our way."
Roberta tells Jack what the phone call was about and they leave the office quickly.

ÜBUNG 4 !

Übung 4: Welche der folgenden Aussagen sind wahr? Markieren Sie mit richtig ✔ oder falsch – !

1. Marco is from Italy. ☐
2. Jack is Roberta's assistant. ☐
3. Roberta is an inspector. ☐
4. Adam Giles is very handsome. ☐
5. Jack hates sport. ☐
6. Jack has short, blond hair. ☐

They arrive fifteen minutes later. Roberta tries the shop door and it opens. As she puts her foot on the doormat, a *bell* starts ringing at the back of the shop. Jack follows Roberta in and both look around the shop. Roberta hears a strange noise and walks to the *counter*. She sees the telephone, but the *receiver* is hanging somewhere behind the *counter*. She *leans* over the *counter* and *catches her breath*.
"Jack!"
"Be patient, Roberta. I haven't found anything yet."
Roberta shouts, "Jack! I've found a *body*. I think it's Giles."
Jack runs behind the *counter*.
"You're right, Roberta. It's Giles. He's dead. Look, you call for *back-up* and I'll stay here with the *body*.
Roberta walks to the door and calls the *emergency services* on her mobile phone. Just as she hangs up, an old woman tries to enter the shop and Roberta blocks her way.

"I'm sorry Madam, but you can't come in here."
"Why not? The sign says 'open' and I need to buy a newspaper."
"*I'm afraid* that's not possible, Madam. This shop is now a *crime scene*."
The old lady put her hand to her mouth. "*Oh dear!* What happened then?"
"Erm... There was an accident, Madam. Could you please leave now?"
"Oh, all right. You should be out *arresting* those dangerous drivers. One left this shop half an hour ago and nearly ran me down. Good-bye."
It takes a few seconds for Roberta to understand what the old woman is saying.
"One moment please, Madam. Could you say that again, please?"
"First you want me to leave and now you want me to stay. You young people don't know what you want."
"Yes. You're right, Madam. Now, could you please repeat what you said?"
"I said: I need to buy a newspaper."
"I don't mean that, Madam. Would you please repeat what you said after that?"

Übung 5: Suchen Sie das Gegenteil der Wörter in Klammern!

ÜBUNG 5 !

"Well. Half an hour ago I was crossing the *zebra crossing* about a hundred *yards* up the street. I saw a car stop (1. inside) ____________ the shop and a man got (2. out) ____________."

"Yes, Madam. What happened then?"

"The driver just raced along the street and nearly knocked me (3. up) __________. He didn't even brake, the hooligan."

"I see, Madam. Did it really take you half an hour to (4. run) ____________ a hundred *yards* to the shop?"

The (5. young) ______________ lady's face reddened.

"Well, I saw Mrs Dowd in her garden, so I had to tell her about my escape from (6. life) _____________."

"I understand, Madam. Can you describe the car or the two (7. women) ____________ please?"

"The car is (8. black) ___________ and quite small. I'm not usually (9. bad) ____________ at *makes*, but it looks the same as my *nephew's*. German, I think. Something to do with sport."

"Do you mean 'Golf', Madam?"
"Yes. That's it."
"What about the men, Madam. Can you describe them for me?"
"Not really. They both have dark hair and aren't pale enough to be Englishmen. I would say Italian or Greek."
"Do you remember the *registration number* of the car, Madam?"
"No. My eyes are not as good as they *used to* be. Although I remember a 'B' *registration*. That's the same as my *nephew's* car, but his is red."
"Well. Thank you very much, Madam. Your information helps me a lot."
"You're welcome. You are a very nice girl. Pretty, too, and so polite. I don't meet many of those *nowadays*. Goodbye, my dear."

Roberta turns and smiles. It's nice to be called a girl again, she thinks. While Roberta is talking to the woman, Jack is looking around the shop. He is very careful not to *disturb* any *evidence*. He finds nothing in the shop and goes through to the back room. It is used as a *storeroom* and has a little *kitchenette*. Dirty dishes with leftover food are lying in the sink and Jack holds his nose in *disgust*. He turns and looks slowly around the room. The first thing he notices is that the table and chairs aren't straight. He's not surprised, because Mr Giles wasn't a very *tidy* person. Then he sees that a corner of the carpet is folded over.

Jack bends down to straighten it and discovers a *handle* built into the wooden floor. He *whistles* and pulls the carpet all the way back. There is a *trapdoor* set into the floor. He *grabs* the *handle* and pulls the *trapdoor* open. There are steps leading down into the darkness. Jack sees a *switch mounted on* the *handrail* and pushes it down. Suddenly there is light and Jack goes down a few steps. His mouth opens in *amazement*. The room is *neat*, clean and organized. The shelves on all four walls are full of weapons and *gadgets* of every *kind*. Jack quickly goes back up the steps and goes outside to look for Roberta.

Police cars are now arriving at the shop, and Roberta shows them where to find the *body*. She is writing down what the old lady said, when Jack comes out of the shop. She tells Jack about the old lady and Jack tells her about his discovery. Then they go back into the *newsagent's*, where Jack shows Roberta where he found the weapons.

Together, they have another look around the shop, to see if they can find any helpful *clues*. However, they find nothing of interest. Then the shop is full of people. A doctor is examining Mr Giles as a grey-haired man *approaches* Roberta and Jack.

"Hello, Inspector Fletcher. Didn't we work together on the murder in the *docks* last year?"
"Yes we did, Mr Harris. How are you?"
"I'm fine thanks, Inspector." He looks at Jack.
"I'm sorry, Mr Harris. This is Jack Walsh, my assistant."
"I'm pleased to meet you, Mr Walsh. Right, we need to start collecting *evidence*, so *I'm afraid* I will have to ask you to leave now."
"We understand, Mr Harris. Goodbye then."
Mr Harris *waves his hand* at them as he opens his *case* full of instruments.
Roberta and Jack decide to go back to the office and try and *trace* the car.

ÜBUNG 6 !

Übung 6: Wählen Sie die richtige Variante aus!

1. Roberta is a very ____________ girl.
   a) ☐ bad
   b) ☐ angry
   c) ☐ nice

2. The table and chairs aren't ____________.
   a) ☐ wood
   b) ☐ straight
   c) ☐ metal

3. This is Jack, my ____________.
   a) ☐ husband
   b) ☐ boyfriend
   c) ☐ assistant

4. I am ______________ to meet you.
   a) ☐ pleased
   b) ☐ lucky
   c) ☐ angry

5. Mr Giles wasn't a very ______________ person.
   a) ☐ happy
   b) ☐ tidy
   c) ☐ satisfied

Jack tells Roberta that there are thousands of white Golfs registered in London, but only 84 have a "B" *registration*. Jack prints the 84 *registration numbers* out and gives Roberta half of them. After ten minutes, Roberta *leans* back in her chair.
"This isn't getting us anywhere, Jack. Can you think of anything else we could try?"
"I have an idea. Why don't we run the 84 names through our criminal *files*? There's a pretty good *chance* that whoever is involved has a *criminal record*."
"Good idea, Jack! Let's do that."

Jack calls up the criminal *files* and tells the computer to search under the *registration numbers* for known criminals. The computer produces five names. Jack then does more checking and finds out that two of the five are in prison and one other is dead.
Roberta and Jack drive to the first address, but there is nobody home and the neighbour tells them that Mr and Mrs Hale are visiting their daughter in Australia. They won't be back for another four weeks.
They drive to the second address, which is in Chelsea. The owner of the car is Ali Ibrahim, a *suspected* criminal. Mrs Ibrahim

answers the door and tells them that she hasn't seen Ali for a few days.

Roberta looks at the woman and can see that she is nervous.

"May we come in, Mrs Ibrahim?"

"Look. I tell you he's not here."

"We would like to come in *anyway*. We don't want the neighbours to hear everything."

Mrs Ibrahim looks at the next house and sees that the curtains are moving.

"Okay. If you must."

Jack and Roberta enter the house.

! ÜBUNG 7

Übung 7: Bringen Sie die Wörter in die richtige Reihenfolge!

1. idea I an have

____

2. names computer five the produces

____

3. answers Ibrahim door the Mrs

____

4. enter and Roberta house the Jack

____

5. shop are at cars now police arriving the

____

Mrs Ibrahim turns to Roberta and Jack.

"Now that you're here, you might as well sit down. Would you like something to drink?"

Roberta sits down and smiles.

"Not for me, thank you."

Mrs Ibrahim looks at Jack and he shakes his head.

Roberta takes out a notepad and pencil.

"Now, Mrs Ibrahim. When was the last time you saw your husband?"

"A few days ago."

"When exactly, Mrs Ibrahim?"

Suddenly there are *screams* from children upstairs. Mrs Ibrahim stands up, but Jack *waves* her back.

"I'll *take care of* them."

He goes up the stairs and Mrs Ibrahim doesn't look happy with the situation.

Roberta continues.

"What *kind of* car does your husband drive?"

"A white one."

"A white what?"

"Oh, I don't know. Something small."

"A Golf, maybe?"

"Yes. I think it's a Golf."

"Where does your husband work?"

"He doesn't."

Roberta looks slowly around the living room.

"You have a lovely house. New stereo, new plasma television and very expensive furniture. Where does all this money come from, Mrs Ibrahim?"

"You ask Ali. I think his family has money."

"That's nice. All right, *that's all for now*."

Mrs Ibrahim jumps up from the couch and runs to the foot of the stairs.

ÜBUNG 8 !

Übung 8: Übersetzen Sie die Farben und enträtseln Sie das Lösungswort!

1. rot □ _ _
2. gelb _ _ _ _ □ _
3. blau □ _ _ _
4. grün _ _ _ □ _
5. braun _ □ _ _ _
6. weiß _ _ _ □ _
7. schwarz _ _ □ _ _

Lösung: _ _ _ _ _ _ _

"Okay, children. You can come down now."
The children come *banging* down the stairs and Jack follows them. At the bottom, Fatima, the girl, *grabs* his hand and smiles at him lovingly.
Mrs Ibrahim picks up the girl and gives Jack a *dirty look.*
Roberta and Jack thank her and go back to their car. Jack starts the *engine* and says, "Jusuf, Mrs Ibrahim's son, is very lucky. His room is full of all the *latest* toys. They must have cost a *fortune*."
"Jack!"
"Where to, Roberta?"
"Switch the *engine* off, Jack."
"Why, Roberta? Did I do something wrong?"
"No Jack, you didn't. I think Mrs Ibrahim is lying to us. She seemed very nervous," Roberta replies.

"Well, I know she is lying. Jusuf told me that his dad was there at breakfast time, but maybe he was lying?"
"*Trust* me, Jack. My *gut feeling* tells me that Mrs Ibrahim knows where her husband is."
"Oh, Roberta. You know I don't believe in that sort of thing," Jack says.
"Look, Jack!"
Jack looks to where Roberta is pointing and sees Mrs Ibrahim, who is now wearing a *headscarf* and sunglasses, leave her house and hurry down the street.
Jack says in *frustration*, "Roberta, how do you do it?"
"It doesn't matter, Jack. She's walking towards the shops, but I don't think that she's going shopping. Look, she's wearing sun-glasses."
"Should we follow her on foot?"
"No, Jack. She would recognize us. We'll follow her with the car, but keep a few hundred *yards* back."
As Mrs Ibrahim turns the corner at the end of the street, Jack starts the car and drives slowly to the corner. They see Mrs Ibrahim cross the street and go into a pub next to a bakery. Jack knows the pub and he tells Roberta that a lot of criminal types meet there.
Jack parks the car outside the pub, and they look through the window. They see Mrs Ibrahim *approach* the bar and speak to a man. Roberta looks at one of the *files* that she brought with her and tells Jack that it's Ali Ibrahim.
Ali is talking angrily to his wife and she starts to cry. Jack *tugs* Roberta's sleeve.
"Look, Roberta. There's a white Golf parked just down the street."
Roberta looks at the *files* in her hands.
"That's the one we are looking for, Jack. It's registered to Ali Ibrahim. Let's call for some *back-up*."

Übung 9: Welche Gegenteile gehören zusammen? Ordnen Sie zu!

1. down	☐ mum
2. top	☐ expensive
3. wrong	☐ laugh
4. dad	☐ arrive
5. leave	☐ bottom
6. cry	☐ right
7. cheap	☐ up

Roberta calls for *assistance* and five minutes later, a green van arrives. A man in blue overalls gets out of the van and goes to the car.

"Excuse me, Madam. Are you Inspector Fletcher?"

"That's right. Are you our *back-up*?"

"Yes, Inspector. I'm *Constable* Simmons."

"Right, *Constable*. Are you alone?"

"No, Inspector. Woman Police *Constable* Kelly is in the van."

"Good. Come on, Jack."

They go to the van and Roberta tells Kelly to take their car back to the station. As she leaves, Mrs Ibrahim comes out of the pub and walks back towards her house. Jack and Roberta are in the back of the van, so they won't be recognized.

"Should I follow her, Inspector?"

"No, *Constable*. We're more interested in her husband."

Two minutes later, Ali Ibrahim leaves the pub, gets into the white Golf and drives off. *Constable* Simmons looks at Roberta.

"Would you like me to catch him, so that you can *arrest* him?"

"No, *Constable*. The *witness* at the *newsagent's* said that there were two foreign-looking men in the car. I'm hoping Mr Ibrahim will lead us to the other one."

The van follows him at a safe distance. Ten minutes later, Ali stops in front of a five-star hotel. He gets out of the car and starts talking to a man at the hotel *entrance*. Roberta is excited.

"Jack, I think that I know him."

"Are you sure, Roberta?"

"Yes. I've seen his face somewhere before."

"Where?"

"That's the problem. I can't remember."

Ali seems very nervous and suddenly turns round and points towards the van. The man talking to Ali looks at the van. Roberta *catches her breath* as his eyes meet hers. She feels like a rabbit in front of a snake.

Suddenly the man *grabs* Ali's arm and pulls him into the hotel. Roberta and Jack jump out of the van and run to the hotel *entrance*. There is no sign of them in the lobby, and Jack asks the receptionist if he saw where the two men went.

The receptionist points to the back of the hotel and tells Jack that the men left through the back door.

Roberta and Jack run to the door. It opens onto a side street behind the hotel. They look up and down the street, but the two men are gone. They walk back to the van and tell the driver to take them back to the station.

Übung 10: Lesen Sie weiter und fügen Sie die Übersetzung der angegebenen Wörter ein!

ÜBUNG 10 !

When they get back to the (1. Büro) ________________, there is a message on Roberta's desk. It's from Mr Harris, the *crime scene investigator*. Roberta should ring him as soon as possible. She calls him (2. sofort) ________________.

"Hello, Mr Harris. It's Roberta Fletcher."

"Ah, Inspector Fletcher! We managed to get a fingerprint off the (3. Tür) ____________ *handle* at the *newsagent's*. It could belong to anyone, but it's (4. wahrscheinlich) ________________ worth running it through your *criminal records*."

"Thanks, Mr Harris. When can you mail it to me?"

"It's already on its way to you."

Roberta's computer (5. zeigt) ________________ a received e-mail and she calls it up. The (6. Fingerabdruck) ________________ is quite clear, and she runs it through the *criminal records*.

A few minutes (7. später) ____________________, "*No matches*" *flashes* on her screen.

Roberta rings the hotel where they lost Ali and asks them to fax her a guest list. She hangs up and looks over at Jack. He is busy looking through some *files*.

"Jack, the fingerprint isn't on the records. I think I'll ring the hospital and see if they have finished the *post-mortem examination* yet."

"Good idea, Roberta. I need a coffee. Would you like one, too?"

"Yes please, Jack."

Jack leaves and Roberta calls the hospital.

"Hello. This is Inspector Fletcher. I'm *in charge of* the Giles murder *case*. Do you know if the *post-mortem* is finished?"

"I think it's still going on. I'll *put you through* to the autopsy room."
"Thanks very much."
"Autopsy room. John Bird speaking."
"Hello, Dr Bird. It's Roberta Fletcher here."
"Hello, Inspector."
"Did you finish the Giles *post-mortem*?"
"We're nearly finished."
"You see, I'm at a *dead end* and I was wondering if you could help? Any information would be *appreciated*."
"As you probably know, he was *strangled*. The interesting thing is that he seems to have been strangled with wire."
"That's interesting. Is it *common*?"
"Not at all. It was a *common* way to kill people twenty years ago, when most killers used *piano wire*, but this is my first since then. I'll send you a copy of the full report in about half an hour."
"That's great, Dr Bird. Thanks a lot."
Roberta puts the phone down as Jack comes back with the coffee. The fax machine starts to print as Jack gives her the coffee.
"Thanks, Jack. I hope that's the guest list from the hotel. Could you go through it, please? I want to run something through the Interpol *file*."
"Sure. No problem."
Roberta calls up the Interpol *files*. Under "method of killing", she types in "wire/*piano wire*". Ten seconds later she gets two *hits*.
The first is: "Jaques Bernod, *assassin*, born Marseilles, France, 1928, died Paris 1982."
The second is: "Marco, *assassin*, is *suspected* of at least five *assassinations*. Price per *assassination* believed to be 1 million dollars, preferred killing method: strangulation with *piano wire*, no further information *available*."
Roberta *claps* her hands.

"Jack! It's Marco. There's a very unclear photo, but it's him. I recognize the eyes."

Jack walks over, grinning.

"Roberta. I recognize this name on the guest list."

"Which one, Jack?"

"This one. Clive Hadley."

"Hadley. Isn't that the millionaire who owns a building company?"

"Yes. Don't you remember? We've been trying to get him for years. We are sure that he's an international *arms dealer*."

"Now I remember. We don't have any *proof*, do we?"

"No, but maybe we can get him this time!"

"I hope so, Jack. Now, you continue checking the guest list and I'll get Clive Hadley's *file*."

! ÜBUNG 11

Übung 11: Beantworten Sie die Fragen zum Text!

1. Does Dr Bird work in the autopsy room?

____

2. Why does Roberta call the hospital?

____

3. Who owns a building company?

____

4. Why does Roberta clap her hands?

____

5. What does Jack get Roberta to drink?

____

6. What does Roberta call up on the Interpol files?

____

When Roberta comes back with Clive Hadley's *file*, Jack *scratches* his head. He tells her that he doesn't recognize any other names on the list.
"What's the connection to Hadley? Do you think Marco is in England to buy weapons off him?"
"I doubt it. He bought weapons from Giles."
"Jack. Look, I have an idea. Perhaps Marco is staying at Ibrahim's house?"
"It's worth checking. In any *case*, Mrs Ibrahim might know where to find him."
"Well, why don't you go over there and ask her?"
"Good idea, Roberta. I'll do it now."
Jack leaves and Roberta continues looking at the *files*. She is interrupted as the phone rings. It is *Constable* Simmons, her van driver. He tells her that he saw where Ali went. She tells him to wait for her at the *entrance* to the building. On the way down, she rings Jack and informs him.

Chapter 3: The Chase

ÜBUNG 12 !

Übung 12: Setzen Sie die Wörter an der richtigen Stelle ein!
(win, sister, photo, sure, man, upstairs, play)

Jack arrives at the Ibrahims' and shows the (1.) ______________ to Mrs Ibrahim.

"Sorry. I don't know this (2.) ____________."

"Are you (3.) ____________, Mrs Ibrahim?"

"Positive."

Just then, Jusuf and his (4.) ____________, Fatima, come running down the stairs. Jusuf sees the photo in Jack's hand."

"Hello, Uncle Jack. What's that?"

"It's a game, Jusuf. Guess who it is and you (5.) ____________ a sweet."

Mrs Ibrahim *grabs* Jusuf.

"Get back (6.) ____________, Jusuf, and take your sister with you."

"No, mummy. I want to (7.) ____________ this game with Uncle Jack."

Jack puts his hand on Mrs Ibrahim's shoulder.
"Let them look, Mrs Ibrahim."
Mrs Ibrahim goes very pale and sits on the couch. Jack takes two sweets out of his pocket and turns to the children.
"Okay. Are you ready?"
They both *nod* and smile. Jack shows them the photo.
"It's Uncle Marco! We win. Give us the sweets!"
Jack gives them the sweets, sends them upstairs and turns to Mrs Ibrahim.
"Okay, Mrs Ibrahim. Now I want the truth, or I will have to *arrest* you and take your children to a children's home."
Mrs Ibrahim *nods* her head *in defeat*.
"I'll give you the address of the *safe house*, but I want you to promise me that Ali won't be hurt."

"I can't do that, Mrs Ibrahim. I can only tell you that the British Police don't hurt people, unless they absolutely have to."
Mrs Ibrahim looks into Jack's eyes, *nods* and tells him the address.

The address is only about two miles away and Jack quickly drives there. It's an old house set back from the road. Jack tries the door, but it's locked. There's a *bell* with no *nameplate* next to the door, so Jack pushes it. Jack hears the *bell* ring inside the house, but nobody answers it. He's just wondering what to do next when he hears a voice.
"Hey, you! What do you want?"
An old man comes from around the back of the house, *wiping* dirt from his hands.
"I'm sorry to *bother* you. I'm a police officer – here's my *badge*. I need to know who lives in this house."
"A man named Ali Ibrahim is renting it for two months."
"Right. Well, I need to search it. You do have a *spare key*, don't you?"
"Of course I do. I'll go and get it."
The old man goes to a car parked in front of the house and gets a bunch of keys from the *glove compartment*. He then lets Jack into the house. He turns to Jack.
"Mr Ibrahim's not in any trouble, is he?"
"Not yet. Listen, Mr...?"
"Devlin, Sam Devlin."
"Mr Devlin. Do you think I could have a few minutes alone to take a look around the flat?"
"Sure. No problem. I'll wait in the garden. Just shout when you're finished."
"Thanks a lot."
Jack walks into the living room, but it's empty except for a couch

and a television. He goes past the kitchen and then through a door, which leads to a small bedroom.

ÜBUNG 13

Übung 13: Welche Wörter passen zusammen? Setzen Sie die richtige Ziffer ein!

1. living	☐ table
2. safe	☐ bell
3. police	☐ phone
4. no	☐ room
5. alarm	☐ compartment
6. glove	☐ officer
7. mobile	☐ problem
8. bedside	☐ house

There is a travel bag with a change of clothes on the bed. The *wardrobe* is empty. He pulls the *drawer* of the bedside table, but it sticks. He takes it out completely and sees an *envelope* taped to the bottom. He opens the *envelope* and sees a long list of weapons, including *rockets*. It's dated the fourth of June 1984 and the customer is a Colonel Jamirez. Jack is pretty sure that this will be the rebels' leader. He *whistles* and looks at the *signature*. It is signed by Clive Hadley. His jacket pocket starts vibrating and he takes out his mobile phone.

"Hello?"

"Jack, it's me, Roberta. Are you at the Ibrahims'?"

"No, but I have *proof* that Hadley is selling weapons. The document shows that he sold weapons to a Colonel Jamirez in 1984."

"Great! So Marco intends to kill Hadley?"

"That's almost certain. Where are you?"

"I'm following Ali's white Golf. Marco's in the car with him and it looks as though they are driving to Waterloo Bridge."
"Just a minute, Roberta. I read in the newspaper that Clive Hadley's building company is doing renovations on Waterloo Bridge."
"Yes, of course. This morning I read that the bridge is being re-opened today."
"What time?"
"I'm quite sure they said 3 p.m."
"It's twenty-five past two now. I'll meet you there. I'm leaving as soon as my *back-up* gets here."
"Okay, Jack, but hurry! Neither of us is *armed*. It would be too dangerous to try and *arrest* Marco and Ali at the moment."
Jack runs out of the house. He shouts thank you to Mr Devlin and gets in his car. He puts the blue light on the roof and drives off *at full speed*.

Meanwhile, Roberta and *Constable* Simmons are following Ali's car in a blue *estate car*. Roberta is sure that Ali knows they are behind him, because he is now driving faster.
"Can't you drive faster, *Constable*?"
"Sorry, Inspector. I can't. I'm driving as fast as I can."
Suddenly a lorry pulls out from a side street and *Constable* Simmons *brakes* very hard. The car *skids* with a *screech* of brakes and crashes into the lorry with a loud bang. Suddenly there is silence. Roberta shakes herself and starts to get out of the car, but the door is stuck. She hears a groan and looks across at *Constable* Simmons. His *forehead* is bleeding quite badly.
"*Constable* Simmons, are you okay?"
"I'm fine, Inspector. It's only a scratch."
"No, it isn't. You are bleeding quite heavily and I think you need *stitches*. I'll call for an ambulance right away."

"No really, Inspector..."

"No arguing, *Constable*. You wait here for the ambulance. That's an order."

"Yes, Inspector."

The traffic is standing still and drivers start *honking* their horns and shouting *abuse*.

As Roberta gets out of the car, a man with grey hair *grabs* her by the arm.

"Are you hurt? I'm a doctor. I can help."

"Doctor, could you *do me a favour*?"

"Yes, of course."

"Can you look after my driver until the ambulance gets here, please?"

"Of course."

"Thank you very much."

"Roberta calls for an ambulance and then calls the station to arrange a road block on Waterloo Bridge. She looks around and sees a motorcyclist talking to the lorry driver. She runs across to them.

"Excuse me!"

The motorcyclist looks her up and down and *obviously* likes what he sees.

"Yes, my love?"

"First, I'm not your love, and second, I'm a police officer. Here's my *identity card*."

"Sorry, officer. How can I help you?"

"I want you to take me to Waterloo Bridge as fast as you possibly can."

"What about *speed traps*?"

"If we get caught, I'll pay them."

"That's *fair enough*, let's go."

Übung 14: Lesen Sie weiter und unterstreichen Sie jeweils die richtige Variante!

ÜBUNG 14 !

Jack races away (1.) to/from the hotel and takes the (2.) slowest/fastest route to Waterloo Bridge. However, he's not in luck, because the rush hour traffic has (3.) begun/ended. He can't get past the cars, even though his blue light is *flashing*. He *curses* that he would probably be faster (4.) swimming/running. This gives him an idea. He thinks he could run to the (5.) pub/bridge in about ten minutes. He (6.) jumps/falls out of the car and starts (7.) running/walking. Behind him the car drivers are *honking* their horns, because Jack's car is now blocking them.
Jack (8.) cries/*grins* and *whispers*, "Sorry."

At the same time, Roberta is holding on to the motorcyclist *for dear life*. Horns are *honking* and drivers are shouting. She hears a woman scream and sees a mother holding her child as the motorcycle rushes past. Now she remembers why she didn't join the Motorcycle Police. She hates motorcycles!

Chapter 4: Showdown on Waterloo Bridge

Ali and Marco are now only half a mile from Waterloo Bridge. Ali looks into the *rearview mirror* every few seconds.
Finally he says, "We lost them, Master."
"Good!"
Ali looks at Marco and sees that he looks very *grim*. Marco checks his gun again for the fifth time.
Ali looks up and sees that in front of them a couple of police cars are blocking the *entrance* to the bridge.

"Master, what should I do?"
"Drive!"
"But, Master?"
Marco *leans* over and presses Ali's right leg down. The car *engine* screams and the car shoots forward.
"Master, no!"
Marco then uses his other hand to *grab* the *steering wheel* and keep the car in a straight line.
Ali puts his hands to his face and starts praying.

The car hits the back of a police car *at full speed* and there is a loud bang. The white Golf is badly damaged, but it is still going very fast. Ali is *unconscious*, but Marco presses his leg down again and steers for a Rolls Royce in the middle of the bridge. A man in a black suit, who is carrying a gun, jumps out of the Rolls Royce and shoots at the Golf. He jumps aside at the last second as the Golf crashes into the Rolls Royce at full force. There is the sound of screeching metal and steam is coming out from under the Golf's bonnet.
Marco dives out of the car holding his gun. He rolls on the ground as the bodyguard moves from behind the Golf. The bodyguard shoots, but Marco is already rolling. He stops, *takes* careful *aim* and shoots the bodyguard. Marco starts to walk to the Rolls Royce and realizes that his right leg doesn't work. He looks down in surprise and sees his trousers are covered in blood. Then the pain comes. But he stumbles on towards the Rolls Royce.
Clive Hadley is sitting in the back and is shaking with fear.
"Who are you? Please don't kill me."
"My name is Marco. You sold *rockets* to Colonel Jamirez twenty years ago. One of those *rockets* killed my family. You have their blood on your hands and you'll die for it."

"Please. You don't have to kill me."
"Give me one reason why I shouldn't, Hadley."
"It was only a business deal."
"It was a business deal that *wiped out* my family and thousands of others."
"I just wanted to make a bit of money."
"A bit of money! You made millions by causing thousands of deaths!" Marco shouts.
Hadley starts begging.
"Marco, please. How much do you want? I'll pay anything you ask. One million, two million? Name your price and the money is yours!"
Marco's pain is now almost *unbearable*, but he smiles.
"You can't buy me, Hadley. You *caused* so much pain and death over the years. Well, now it's your turn."
Marco sees the fear disappear from Hadley's face and, at the same time, hears a noise behind him. He turns around.

Übung 15: Enträtseln Sie die folgenden Definitionen!

1. The people who arrest criminals. *police* (eoclpi)
2. Mum, dad, brother, sister. ____________ (lamfyi)
3. The motor of a car. ____________ (inegen)
4. Someone who protects people. ____________ (uoydgabrd)
5. The number one plus six zeros. ____________ (lnilomi)
6. It has two wheels and an engine. ____________ (bomroteki)
7. If you are suddenly gone, you ... ____________ (paesidpra)

Roberta and Jack arrive at the *entrance* to the bridge at the same time. Jack is breathing heavily and Roberta is feeling very *dizzy* from the motorcycle ride.

They both turn to look at the scene on the bridge. There seem to be smashed and smoking cars everywhere.

Roberta can see Marco *leaning* into the Rolls Royce talking to somebody. Out of the corner of her eye she sees movement. There is a man in a dark suit who is *creeping* very slowly from behind the Rolls Royce. He has a gun in his hand and is walking towards Marco!

She knows she shouldn't, but she really wants to shout a warning to Marco. Before she can react, there is a loud *scream*.

"Hey!"

It's Ali. He is standing in front of the Golf and shouting to *distract* the bodyguard.

There is the sound of two gunshots, and Marco and the bodyguard fall to the ground. The bodyguard doesn't move, but Marco *crawls* back towards the Rolls Royce.

Clive Hadley panics and tries to get out of the car on the side away from Marco, but the door has been blocked by the crash.

Roberta, Jack and Ali start running towards Marco shouting for him to stop.

Marco ignores them and with the last of his *strength*, pulls himself to the door of the car.

Clive Hadley is still trying to open the car door. His face is covered in sweat and he's calling for his mother. Suddenly he sees Marco's head appear at the other door and he screams.

"Marco, no! Please have *mercy*!"

Marco, his face full of pain, shakes his head sadly.

"No *mercy*, Hadley. *Revenge* is mine!"

He shoots Hadley in the head and falls back onto the floor.

Roberta kneels down next to Marco's *body*, when suddenly Marco coughs and opens his eyes. He smiles through his pain.
"The police, I *presume*?"
"That's right, Marco."
"I was right to kill Hadley. There is *proof* in my room at the *safe house*."
"We got it, Marco."
Marco tries to laugh, but it turns into a cough and blood runs from his mouth.
"Don't talk, Marco. The ambulance is coming."
"Too late. I can already hear her voice."
"Whose?"
"My sister's. Jasmin..."
Roberta feels Marco's *body* relax and *wipes* a tear from her eye.

A NICE NEIGHBOURHOOD

Sarah Trenker

Chapter 1: A Meeting in the Church

It is cold in the *church hall* and their breath comes out in little clouds. Detective Frank Durham pulls up the collar of his leather jacket and *glances* at his partner. Barry smiles and just *shrugs his shoulders*.

None of the six men around the table speak. They just wait. Police *Constable* Jones, Dr Sterling, Mr Monks and Mr Philips sit on one side of the table, the two detectives on the other. The only person missing is the *mayor*.

Barry wishes he had a bigger chair. He is a heavy man and his wooden chair *creaks* loudly as he tries to find a more comfortable position.

"How much longer do you think the *mayor* is going to be?" asks Frank impatiently. "Wouldn't it be better to call him?"

"I already have," replies Mr Monks. "He said he was in the middle of another meeting and would come as quickly as he could."

"We could start without him," suggests Mr Philips.

"No, no, Mr Ainsley wouldn't like that," the *constable* replies.

At last the door opens and the *mayor* walks in. With his long, dark-blue coat over his suit, and an umbrella in his hand, he looks more like a London *stockbroker* than a village *mayor*. Frank dislikes him immediately.

"Sorry I am late," says the *mayor* in a voice that does not sound sorry at all.

He walks over to the table. "You must be Detectives Durham and Andrews, I *presume*," he says and smiles at his little joke.

Übung 1: Steigern Sie die folgenden Adjektive. Beachten Sie die Beispiele im Text!

1. big ________________ ________________
2. comfortable ________________ ________________
3. heavy ________________ ________________
4. cold ________________ ________________
5. good ________________ ________________
6. slow ________________ ________________

"And you are Mark Ainsley, the VILLAGE *mayor*, I *presume*," answers Frank dryly.

"Just so, just so," says the *mayor*. The smile dies on his lips as he reads Frank's *expression*. "As I said, sorry you had to wait. Let's *get straight down to business*."

He sits down and Barry opens his notebook on a clean page.

Frank is about to speak when the *mayor* interrupts him. "Perhaps you should just ask us the questions and we can tell you all we know, can't we?" He looks round at the other men who all *nod*.

Frank takes another breath.

"On the other hand", continues the *mayor* and places his hands in front of him, "it might be easier if we just told you what we know. What would you prefer?"

"I think, *mayor*, if you don't mind, I'll ask the questions," Frank says quickly before the *mayor* can come up with a third choice.

"Now, my information so far is that three men have died here in

Little Meadow in the course of the last two months. The last man, Michael Reed, died on Monday. Is that right?"
"Yes, Monday evening," replies PC Jones.
"And after this third death you began to wonder about the causes of the deaths of Nicholas Fields and Tony Edmonton, is that right?"
"Yes."
"Dr Sterling, you signed the *death certificates* of all three men, I believe. What made you change your opinion about the cause of death?"
"I knew all three men," answers the doctor. "They were all patients of mine at one time or another. They had stress at work like a lot of men of their age but otherwise were in the best of health. So when the third one died, it seemed too much of a *coincidence*."
"And that is why you *reported* your *suspicions* to the *mayor*?"
"Yes."
"Did you do a *post-mortem examination* on any of the men?"
"No. I am a *general practitioner*; I can't really do a *proper post-mortem*. However, I did notice that all of the corpses had yellow tongues. At first, I just thought it was because of *rigor mortis*, but now I am not so sure."
Frank looks at Barry. "You saw enough *bodies* when you worked with that team in London. Is a yellow tongue a typical sign of *rigor mortis*?"
"Not really," answers Barry. "I think we should let one of the doctors in town look at the *bodies*."
"*BODY*," corrects the *mayor*. "We *cremated* Nicholas Fields and Tony Edmonton."
"Oh great!" *mutters* Frank.
"Well, they weren't *church-goers*, you see," explains the *mayor*. "And there is so little space in the *graveyard*. *Anyway* – the men were all new in the village."

"New?" Barry is surprised. "When I spoke to PC Jones on the phone yesterday, he told me that they all moved to Little Meadow about two years ago."
"That still makes them new to this village," answers the *mayor*. "Most of the families who live here have been here for generations. We have a very *close-knit community*."
"So close that you don't like NEW people moving into the village?" asks Frank.
"No, no, that's not what I meant." The *mayor* looks a little embarrassed.

Übung 2: Lesen Sie weiter und unterstreichen Sie die englische Übersetzung der Wörter in Klammern!
(1. schlank, 2. Metzger, 3. stirbt, 4. Plakate, 5. Fall, 6. unterbricht)

Frank *changes the subject*. "Where is Michael Reed now?"
Mr Philips, a red-faced man who manages to make even Barry look slim, holds up a hand the size of a small football. "He's in my fridge. I'm the village butcher. When somebody dies, we always put them in my fridge. It is easier. That way we don't have to drive them to the next town and then back again."
"Yes, that is more practical." Frank suddenly feels like he is in some *kind of* historical novel. It is all too *weird*. There is a butcher who is also the *undertaker*, a friendly policeman who says he doesn't own a gun, and a *mayor* who acts like a king. The village is so small that there isn't even a post office. And if the posters outside the church were anything to go by, the Christmas play is a big *annual* event... He looks over at Mr Monks.
"Mr Monks, what do you know about this *case*?"
A man of only about 25, Mr Monks has a face that already shows

! ÜBUNG 2

the first *wrinkles* of *frustration* – and it is easy to see that he is not happy with life. When he speaks it is like listening to a slow *whine*. "I knew the three men well. I *used to* work for a bank in Gorleston-on-Sea. The three were all investment experts and..."
"Investment experts?" interrupts Frank. "What do you mean by 'investment experts'? Did they work at the bank, too?"

"No, they didn't," answers Mr Monks *irritably*. "They drove round all the villages here. They provided people with investment tips."
"Investment tips?"
Mr Monks sighs as if it is so hard to deal with such idiots. "Yes. You know, it's when someone comes to your home and tells you how to invest your *savings* to get the most out of the money."
Mr Monks pauses. "Or at least that is what good investment experts do."
"Which these three weren't?" Frank *senses* that he is about to learn a possible motive.
Before Mr Monks can continue, however, the *mayor* interrupts him. "Now, now, Mr Monks. There is no need to *bother* the detectives with all of that unless we know that someone really did murder them."
He turns to Frank. "Detective Durham, the fact that the three men were not particularly popular in the village was also something that made Dr Sterling and me *suspicious*. But perhaps it would be better to discuss that after your people have examined Mr Reed's *body*. Otherwise there is really no need for us to *wash our dirty linen in public*."
The *mayor* gives Mr Monks a warning look and the younger man *frowns*, but doesn't say anything else.
Not all perfect in this village then after all, thinks Frank with slight *amusement*. He stands up.

"Well, gentlemen, thank you for your time. I shall send a car over to collect Mr Reed from Mr Philips first thing tomorrow morning. We should have the results of the *post-mortem* by the afternoon."
"Will you phone us?" asks the *mayor*.
"Yes."

Übung 3: Formulieren Sie Fragen mit ***used to*** *zu folgenden Sätzen!*

ÜBUNG 3 !

1. Mr Monks now works for a company in Norwich.

Where did he use to work?

2. I can now drive to work because I have a car.

How ______________________________

3. The detectives can now contact each other with their mobile phones.

How ______________________________

4. The village didn't have a post office until 1991.

Where ______________________________

5. During the summer Mr Philips received his patients in the village hall.

When ______________________________

6. Barry now plays golf in his spare time, but that wasn't always his favourite game.

Which ______________________________

PC Jones walks out to the car with them. "It seems so hard to believe that there could be a murderer living here," he says.
He *waves his hand* at the quiet village streets and the fields in the background. "There hasn't been a murder here since 1924."
In the car, Barry pulls the *safety belt* over his stomach and sits back gratefully into the comfortable seat.
"Strange people, aren't they?" he *chuckles*.
Frank *grins* and rubs his hands together to try and get them warm. "They certainly are."
"Do you think it was murder?" replies Barry.
Frank starts the car. "Oh, I think so. Three healthy but unpopular men suddenly die in a village that doesn't like strangers. That certainly sounds like the perfect *ingredients* for murder to me."
They take the long *winding* road back through the fields and small villages towards the town. For half an hour, they see *nothing* on the road *but* a tractor and three girls on ponies.
Barry is *puzzled*. "Why would three investment experts come and live out in the middle of the East Anglian countryside, I wonder?"
"*Easy pickings* probably," answers Frank, as he lights yet another cigarette. "A lot of hard-working people with money they don't know what to do with!"

ÜBUNG 4 !

Übung 4: Trifft die Aussage zu? Markieren Sie mit richtig ✔ oder falsch – !

1. The name of the village the detectives visit is Little Meadow. ☐
2. It is boiling hot in the church hall. ☐
3. Detective Durham likes the mayor. ☐
4. Mr Monks worked for a bank in Great Yarmouth. ☐

5. The names of the three murdered men are:
Michael Reed, Nicholas Fields and Tony Edmonton. ☐
6. The village undertaker is also the village butcher. ☐

Chapter 2: Dirty Linen

Frank's office is chaotic. There are papers everywhere, photos of criminals on the wall and a bin full of empty cigarette packets and pizza boxes. He and Barry are reading a report about a *theft* in a restaurant in Great Yarmouth when someone knocks on the door.

"Come in," shouts Frank.

Ann Forest walks in. She is the *pathologist* and she and Frank *get on* very well.

"Hi, you two, I've got the results for you."

"And?" says Barry. He puts down the report he has in his hand and stands up to offer Ann his chair. She looks around and shakes her head.

"I'm not sitting down in this *pigsty*. Goodness knows what sort of bacteria are hiding in this room," she says and *grins*.

"Have it your own way," answers Frank, who also *grins*. "So, was it murder?"

"Oh yes, it was certainly murder. *Poison*."

"And what sort of *poison* was it?" Frank asks, suddenly serious.

"Rat *poison*," answers the young *pathologist*.

"You mean like warfarin?" asks Barry.

"Yes," answers Ann. "Although not many people use warfarin today because there are a lot of better alternatives on the market. But there was some warfarin in the *victim's* system, so that might help you if you find someone with it."

"Wouldn't a person know if they *swallowed* rat *poison*?"

"Oh no! Mixed in a cup of tea, for example, the *victim* would not notice a thing – well, until later. Funnily enough, doctors now use warfarin for people with heart problems – *obviously* in small *doses*."

"And Mr Reed's *dose*?" Frank types W-A-R-F-A-R-I-N into the search engine as he asks Ann the question.

Ann has a look at her notes. "Absolutely deadly... Mr Reed *swallowed* enough to kill at least five men. *Anyway*, you can read all you need to know about warfarin in my notes here. It is a very effective *poison*. It *dissolves* in water and, as I said, anyone who takes it will not taste it."

Barry looks down into his mug of tea. "You mean I could be drinking it now and would not know about it?"

"That's right," replies Ann and *grins* again.

Frank stands up and takes the notes from the *pathologist*. "Anything else you can tell us about the *body*?"

"Yes. The *body* looks a bit like an *Egyptian mummy*. That is very typical of rat *poison*. It *dehydrates* the *victim*. Normally, if a *victim* gets to a hospital quickly enough, it is possible to save him. But Mr Reed's stomach also contained a lot of sleeping powder. Mr Reed probably didn't know anything about the *poison* until he found himself in front of *St Peter's gates*."

"*Assuming*, of course, that he went to heaven," replies Frank dryly.

"Exactly!"

ÜBUNG 5 !

Übung 5: Welches Wort ist das „schwarze Schaf"?

1. tidy, clean, chaotic, washed
2. full, nothing, empty, unfilled
3. heart, brain, football, stomach

4. pigsty, pond, house, zoo
5. cocktail, juice, tea, meal
6. thief, policeman, pathologist, detective

After Ann leaves his office, Frank reaches for the phone. He *dials* the number the *mayor* gave him. A secretary answers the phone.
"This is Detective Durham. I would like to speak to Mark Ainsley, please."
"Ah yes, Detective. The *mayor* is expecting your call. I shall *put you through*."
"Good afternoon, Detective Durham. Mark Ainsley speaking. Have you got the results for us?"
"Yes. You were right to be *suspicious*. It was murder."
"Oh *damn*!" *exclaims* the *mayor*. "So what do we do now?"
"Detective Andrews and I will come back to the village tomorrow and start the *investigation*. It would be very helpful if you could get your secretary to make a photocopy of all the information you have about the three men, their addresses, date of arrival in the village, job, and so on."
"Yes, yes, of course," answers the *mayor*. "There is a room here that you can use, if you wish. We don't really have a *proper* police station or village hall here. I have an office on the ground floor of my house. There are two rooms. Police *Constable* Jones uses one of the rooms for his papers but, as you know, we all have a number of different jobs. I earn my money as a *horse breeder*..."
"Yes, I know," answers Frank impatiently, who does not wish to hear another list of all the jobs the *villagers* do.
"I'm only *reminding you*", answers the *mayor* in a snobbish voice, "because I have to drive to Norwich tomorrow morning to sell a couple of horses. Miss Robins, my secretary, will let you in and show you the office, but you will be on your own until the afternoon."

"That will not be a problem, Mr Ainsley," says Frank, happy that he is going to have a *chance* to look through the information about the three men without the *mayor* around.
"I'll see you tomorrow afternoon then."
Frank puts the phone down and looks at Barry. "Can you look through the *press archives* and see if you can find out anything about the three investment experts – or any investment scandals recently? It is time to examine the dirty linen!"
Barry *nods*. "Right you are. I'll get down to it straight away."

! ÜBUNG 6

Übung 6: Lesen Sie weiter und unterstreichen Sie die im Kontext richtige Variante!

Punctually at 9 a.m. the following morning, Frank and Barry walk up the concrete steps of the *mayor's* house and (1.) ring/dial the door-bell. A young secretary with red hair and a big smile opens the door. "Are you the two detectives here to find out which of us is a (2.) *church-goer*/murderer?" she shouts.
"That's right, Miss Robins. That's us," Franks says, smiling at this welcome.
"Come in, please. I'll show you the office."
She leads them to a small office at the back of the house. It is not big, but it is very (3.) light/dark and has a nice view of the garden. "I have put everything I could find about the men on the table," Miss Robins remarks and points to some (4.) clothes/papers. "There is also a list of everyone in the village and their telephone numbers. Mr Ainsley says you are welcome to use the phone for local calls."
"Perfect. That is very kind of him."
"Would you like a coffee?"

"Yes, please. That would be great."
While Miss Robins goes to (5.) bring/get the coffee, Frank and Barry look through the papers on the table.
"*According to* these (6.) photos/documents, they all arrived in the village at the same time," says Barry.
"And they were partners," adds Frank. "They set up their partnership twelve years ago in Lowestoft and then moved here two years ago."
"Hey, look (7.) at/on this!" Barry holds up a photocopy of a page in a newspaper. "This (8.) shows/tells that the rich farmers were not the only reason the three partners moved out here."

Frank takes the cutting from Barry and quickly looks through it. There is a big headline: *Suspicion* of *malpractice*. Underneath it there was a long text about three men who had appeared before the *magistrate* in Lowestoft.
"This says the men got lots of old people to invest in life *insurance* that was only any good for young people. That means the only people helped by the *insurance payments* were the *insurance* company and the investment experts. Apparently some *insurance* companies pay particularly high *commission* for such *contracts*."
"Disgusting," *mutters* Barry and *frowns*.
At that moment Miss Robins comes into the room with the coffee. She sees the photocopy in Frank's hands.
"Yes, a nice trio, weren't they?"
"Did people here know about this when the three moved here?" asks Frank.
Miss Robins puts the *tray* of coffee on the table and *frowns*. "No, of course not. That's why they all moved out here. These men knew country people are very *trusting* and that they could just carry on where they had left off."

Miss Robins *snorts* angrily.

"My grandma lost a lot of money. She has real difficulties paying for her shopping now."

"So there was quite a bit of *bad feeling* towards the men?" Frank *observes*.

"*Bad feeling*! *Hatred* would be a better word." Miss Robins bangs the milk jug on the table next to the two mugs of coffee and the sugar.

"Didn't people try to do anything about it?" asks Barry.

"Yes and no," answers Miss Robins. "It was a long time before people realized what had happened. Then it was too late. *Anyway*, there was nothing that anyone could do. They didn't do anything illegal. It is not as if they held a gun to people's heads. We are simple country people. We tend to believe what people say to us."

Barry *nods* sympathetically.

"So a lot of people lost money to them."

"Yes. All of the pensioners in the village, well, except Mrs Hutchinson, and a lot of younger people, too."

"Well, surely life *insurance* isn't bad for younger people," suggests Barry.

Miss Robins sighs. "Yes, that is why the three did not sell life *insurance* to them. They got them interested in some sort of *property* investment that went very wrong."

"*Property* investment?"

Miss Robins *shrugs*. "I don't know much about it. You'll have to ask the *mayor*, or you could ask my neighbour Fiona Chambers. She *used to* work for Paul & Son Architects. She was in love with Nicholas Fields, but he didn't love her. He just used her to get the information he wanted. She even invested some of her money in his projects. And then, of course, there was Mr Monks. You met him yesterday, I believe?"

"Yes, that right," Frank replies.
"Mr Monks lost his job at the bank in Gorleston-on-Sea because of the three of them," Miss Robins continues. "He really hated them – not that I think he is *capable of* murder," she adds quickly.
Frank *nods*. "I still think it would be good to speak to him and Miss Chambers," he says. "When is a good time to see them?"
Miss Robins *shrugs her shoulders* again. "Anytime really. They are both still looking for new jobs, so they are at home a lot of the time."
Frank looks at Barry, who is *sipping* his coffee. "A good place to start, perhaps? We can go and talk to Miss Chambers and Mr Monks now and be back in time to talk to the *mayor* when he gets back from Lowestoft."

Übung 7: Finden Sie die Synonyme und setzen Sie die richtige Ziffer ein!

ÜBUNG 7

1. hate	☐ cup
2. murder	☐ remark
3. mug	☐ three people
4. happen	☐ dislike
5. say	☐ take place
6. trio	☐ kill

"Hardly a lot going on here, is there?" remarks Frank, as he and Barry walk down the main street to where the *mayor's* secretary said they would find Miss Chambers.
There is one car parked outside the small shop next to the butcher's. Inside the shop, Frank and Barry can see a smart *elderly* lady talking to the young shop assistant.

"I don't think that shop assistant would survive for very long in a busy supermarket in Norwich," *chuckles* Barry in reply.
As they pass the shop, the *elderly* lady customer comes trotting out of the shop towards them. She walks with a stick but holds her back very straight. She smiles *brightly* at the detectives.
"Good morning, young men, my name is Mrs Hutchinson. I hear you are here to find our murderer. How exciting! Of course, I know a lot about the three gentlemen, so do let me know if you need to ask me any questions. I am sure I can help you."
Frank is amused. News *obviously* travels very fast here.
He looks at Mrs Hutchinson and smiles. "We have only just started the *investigation*. But, yes, thank you for your offer. Where do you live, Mrs Hutchinson?"
"Just over there in the blue house," she answers, and points to the house with her stick.
"Would four o'clock be a good time for us to come round?" asks Frank politely.
"If you come around four, you can have tea with me. But please don't keep me waiting, young man. I like to eat at the same time every day. My *digestion* isn't what it was."
Frank *nods* and tries not to laugh. "If we are going to be late, I will let you know, Mrs Hutchinson," he says and watches the old lady walk slowly across the road to the blue house on the other side.

Chapter 3: You Can't Choose Your Neighbours

The little brown cat playing on the sofa is more enthusiastic about the *presence* of the two detectives than Miss Chambers is. A *middle-aged* woman with a big nose and no taste in lipstick, Miss Chambers offers them tea but does not seem to want to speak.

In the *lounge*, Frank remains standing. “Thank you for seeing us *at such short notice*, Miss Chambers,” he says.
“It is my duty,” answers Miss Chambers and *frowns* unhappily.
“Quite right,” *mutters* Frank. “Can you tell us how you knew the three *victims*?”
Miss Chambers *sniffs*. “I’m sure you already know that I was in love with Nicholas Fields. He asked me to marry him.”
The woman brushes some *imaginary crumbs* off the table before she continues. “We met when I worked for Paul & Son Architects. Nicholas seemed such a wonderful man.”
Detective Durham lifts an eyebrow to *pretend* interest.
“Were you still *engaged* at the time of his death, Miss Chambers?”
“No.”
“Why?”
“When I decided to change jobs so I could have more time for him, Nicholas suddenly changed. I thought he would be happy to hear that I had a new job that meant I could be home by 6 p.m. – but he wasn’t. He said it was boring because I no longer had anything exciting to talk about.” Miss Chambers *sniffs* again, this time more loudly.
“What did he find so exciting about hearing you talk about your job with the architects?” Frank asks *gently*.
“He wanted to know what sort of projects we had and whether there was any new business coming to the area. I thought it was because he wanted to find out how much I understood about his business – but I was wrong. I realized later that it was simply because he wanted to use the information I gave him for some new investment scheme he and his friends had thought up. He laughed at me when I told him I was in love with him and that I thought he wanted to marry me. He said I was a silly *old maid* who didn’t know the difference between an innocent flirt and true love. He packed up all

of my things from his house and left them on my doorstep, would you believe?"

Miss Chambers *sniffs* again. "But although I hated him and his partners, I didn't kill them," she adds. "*Anyway*, how did they die?"

"*Poison*," answers Frank.

"*Serves them right!*" *comments* Miss Chambers, with a satisfied *expression* on her face.

Embarrassed, Barry coughs. "I need a glass of water," he says and stands up. "May I get one in the kitchen?"

Miss Chambers *nods* and Barry walks through into the kitchen. For a moment the only sound is of running water as Barry turns the *tap* on in the kitchen.

Frank tries to *change the subject* a bit. "Do you know if either Michael Reed or Tony Edmonton had girlfriends?"

"None of them had steady girlfriends. Nicholas laughed and said that perhaps I would make an honest man of him after all. He and his friends laughed a lot when he said that. Now I know *the joke was on me*."

Barry walks back in and sits down. He looks slightly pale. "I see you have a big bag of rat *poison* in the kitchen. Do you have problems with rats here?"

Miss Chambers is surprised and quite *obviously annoyed* at a question which shows Barry has been looking around her kitchen. "Yes, we all do. That is the disadvantage of living out in the middle of the countryside between fields on one side and a *stream* on the other. The rat population is *enormous* here. Last year I had a family of them in my big flowerpot in the garden. At night they *used to* come out and play with one another. It was impossible to sleep. That was why I bought the warfarin. It's good stuff – and has certainly *solved* a few rat problems for me!"

There is something *menacing* about the way Miss Chambers says "rat problems" and Frank feels a *shiver* go down his *spine*. He looks at Barry and *nods* to show that he is ready to go.

Übung 8: Lesen Sie weiter and setzen Sie die Wörter in Klammern in die passende Lücke ein!
(hesitates, biscuits, House of Commons, lonely, husband, job applications, friends)

Outside, Barry *chuckles*. "She *reminds me of* that story of Nancy Astor and Winston Churchill," he says as they walk back down towards the high street.

"Nancy Astor?"

"Yes. She was the first female member in the (1. Britisches Unterhaus) ______________________. She and Winston Churchill loved to argue. She once said to him, 'If I were your wife, I would put *poison* in your coffee', to which Winston Churchill replied, 'If I were your (2. Ehemann) ____________, I would drink it!'"

Laughing, the two detectives walk on to Mr Monks's home in Shepherd Street.

Thankfully, Mr Monks does not offer them coffee, tea or (3. Kekse) ____________. Instead he asks them to sit at his table in the kitchen. There are lots of (4. Bewerbungen) ________________ lying on the table.

"Perhaps you can tell us how you lost your job at the bank?" Frank asks.

"*Stupidity*, really," answers Mr Monks, the lines of *frustration* deepening in his face. "It can get a bit (5. einsam) ____________ out here when you are single. Tony Edmonton started to invite me round for drinks with his two (6. Freunde) ____________. They talked about their work and were also very interested in my work. It was nice to have someone to talk to..." Mr Monks (7. zögert) ____________.

He *wipes* his brow and then continues. "To start with, I didn't realize they just wanted information from me so they could do a bit of *insider trading*. By the time I did realize, it was too late. When I went to tell my boss about the three of them, he just thought I wanted to *save my own skin*. He *fired me anyway*. I shall never be able to work in a bank again."

"What did Mr Edmonton and the others say when you told them you no longer had a job?" Frank questions.

Mr Monks *frowns*. "They were sympathetic. They even took me out for a meal, but that was it. From one day to the next the phone calls stopped. When I phoned, they suddenly didn't have time for me."

"And how often did you see them after the meal?" Frank watches a nervous *twitch* on the young man's cheek.

"In a small village like this, you see everyone regularly – whether you want to or not," *mutters* Mr Monks. "I often saw the three of them driving through the village or in the shop. They would say hello, but that was it."

Mr Monks starts to write angrily in the corner of one of the *applications*. Suddenly he looks up and *stares* directly at Frank. “Those three *caused* a lot of trouble here. We should have listened to Mrs Hutchinson. She said they meant trouble – and she was right!”

“Hmm. Just one more question, Mr Monks. We hear that most people in Little Meadow have problems with rats. Is that true?”

“Er yes, yes that’s right,” Mr Monks answers. “The last couple of winters have been very warm. Rats are also very intelligent. If one rat eats some *poison* and dies, the others will not touch the *poison*. It’s only very silly rats that eat warfarin in this area. We’ve all been trying out some new stuff recently.”

“And can you tell me what that is? Barry, please write it down.”

Barry gets out his notebook.

“Brodifacoum – B-R-O-D-I-F-A-C-O-U-M. It is good because the rats just *dehydrate* very slowly, so even if they do die somewhere in the house, there is no smell.”

Übung 9: Vervollständigen Sie die folgenden Sätze mit den Wörtern in Klammern!

(mayor, wearing, poison, lives, papers)

1. Detective Durham learns that it is rat ___________ that killed the three investment experts.
2. Mark Ainsley is the ___________ of Little Meadow.
3. Miss Chambers ___________ in Hill Road.
4. She is ___________ a green cardigan when she opens the door.
5. The table in Mr Monks’s kitchen has a lot of ___________ on it.

When Frank and Barry get back to the house, the *mayor* comes out to greet them. Today he is the picture of a country gentleman: *tweed* jacket, brown cord trousers and a thick cotton shirt with a green tie.

"Hello, gentlemen! How are things going? Miss Robins tells me you have been to see Miss Chambers and Mr Monks. Could they help you at all?"

"They certainly made it clear how unpopular the three were in the village," answers Frank. He looks hard at the *mayor*. Although he finds it hard to like this *self-important* little man, a *gut feeling* tells him that the *mayor* has nothing to do with the murders. The *mayor* looks a little uncomfortable when he sees Frank *staring* at him.

Frank looks away. "Excuse me, Mr Ainsley. I *was miles away* for a moment. Do you have time to answer a few questions?"

The *mayor's* face relaxes and he straightens his back. "But of course, Detective Durham! I would be delighted to help you in any way I can."

An hour and a half later, the two detectives come out of the *mayor's* office and walk through the house to the office at the back.

ÜBUNG 10 !

Übung 10: Bringen Sie die Wörter in die richtige Reihenfolge!

1. comes the greet out mayor to them

____

2. show frustration deep his wrinkles

____

3. Durham not like Detective the mayor very much does

____

4. finds the warfarin Chambers's Miss detective kitchen in

____

5. he insider of the manager bank Mr when learned fired the Monks trading

____

____

In the small office, the two detectives are silent for a few minutes. The *mayor* was a man who loved the sound of his own voice. He also knew about everything in the town. He told them that the "terrible three", as he called them, managed to *bankrupt* whole families.

"What surprises me", says Barry, "is that the three continued to live here after people began to find out what happened."

"Yes," agrees Frank and *scratches* his head. "Although the *mayor* said he didn't see them again after that article appeared in the local paper. That might be important. Can you phone Police *Constable* Jones, Mr Philips and Dr Sterling? Ask them if they remember when they last saw the three men alive."

Barry picks up a list of telephone numbers and walks over to the phone.

Frank stands by the window and thinks for a minute. Then he pulls out his mobile phone and rings the *pathologist* at the police station.

"Hi, Ann, it's Frank. Have you got a moment?"

"Sure, Frank. What's up?"

"How long does it take for rat *poison* to kill a rat?"

"That depends on the *dose*. Sometimes death can be very slow and

painful if a rat doesn't eat much of the *poison*. Why do you ask?"
"Oh, just a little *hunch* of mine. I'll tell you about it when we get together next week. Thanks again for your help."
"No problem. Always glad to help."
The line goes dead and Frank continues to look out of the window while Barry talks to the *villagers*.
Five minutes later, Barry puts down the phone. "Well, I've spoken to all of them. None of them remembers seeing the three after the newspaper article."
"And the article appeared in July sometime, didn't it?"
Barry picks up the photocopy of the newspaper article. "Yes, that's right."
"Which would mean about four weeks before Mr Edmonton died and about eight weeks before Michael Reed died."
"So? What's the connection?" Barry looks at Frank. He knows that *expression*. Frank knows something he doesn't.
"I think we should visit Mr Reed's house. I'm beginning to think these three little rats had to pay a lot for the cheese they stole. Ask Miss Robins to give us the key so we can go straight there tomorrow morning. Then we should *get our skates on* – otherwise we will be late for tea with Mrs Hutchinson!"

ÜBUNG 11 !

Übung 11: Wie heißt der Infinitiv? Setzen Sie die Grundform der folgenden Verben ein!

1. told ______	4. thought ______
2. stole ______	5. knew ______
3. began ______	6. could ______

Chapter 4: Tea and Biscuits at Home

It takes a while for Mrs Hutchinson to open the door. She smiles happily at the two detectives. "Exactly on time. That is very good of you. I know how hard it is for people to be punctual these days. Come in, come in. Don't stand out in the cold. You can leave your shoes in the hall."

The two detectives smile at each other as they take off their shoes and then follow Mrs Hutchinson. A silver teapot and three cups and saucers are already on the table, next to a plate of biscuits.

In order not to be rude, Frank and Barry sit on either side of Mrs Hutchinson and accept a cup of rather watery tea and a biscuit.

"So young men, how are you getting on?" asks Mrs Hutchinson. "I know you have been to see my friends Miss Chambers and Mr Monks. Such nice people. *Nasty* business for both of them. I don't know how they could *trust* such horrible men."

Frank picks up a biscuit. "Mr Monks said you never liked the three men. Perhaps you could tell us why that was?"

Mrs Hutchinson gives Frank a *napkin* and *stirs* her tea. "I worked as a teacher, so I recognize *trouble-makers* immediately."

"You said you knew quite a lot about the three men," says Frank.

"Yes, I do. I like to do a bit of detective work myself," Mrs Hutchinson replies seriously, so that neither Barry nor Frank *dare to* smile. "When I heard about their investment ideas, I realized they were up to no good. How can anyone sell life *insurance* to old people?" She sighs. "Of course, they *took advantage of* the people here. I tried to warn people, but it is difficult when you have no real *proof*. So, for a while, I did nothing, but when Mr Monks lost his job and then Nicholas Fields was so horrible to Miss Chambers, I knew it was time to do something. That's when I came up with the idea of going to the library in Norwich to do some *research* on the Internet."

Barry looks so surprised that Mrs Hutchinson laughs.
"I know. It is difficult to imagine someone like me on a computer. But there is a very nice girl at the library who taught me how to use the search engines. Now I always spend time on the Internet when I visit Norwich."
"And..." asks Frank, hoping that Mrs Hutchinson will get back to what she found out about the three men.
"It was there that I found a small piece about the scandal in Lowestoft. Not very much, but enough to want to know more. The following day I went to Lowestoft and visited the owner of the local paper. What a nice man. He had all the articles about the *case* on his computer. He printed them out for me and I took them straight to the *mayor*."
Barry takes yet another biscuit, but *blushes* when he sees Mrs Hutchinson *staring* at him.
"Eat up, eat up, Detective Andrews. You look like a man who likes his food," she *observes* with a smile. "If you come tomorrow, I shall get a chocolate cake."
"What happened when the people in the village knew about the scandal in Lowestoft? Can you remember?" Frank asks.
She surprises him when she turns round quickly and he sees what for a second almost looks like anger in her bright blue eyes. "Of course I can remember! I'm not senile! The young men didn't think they would have any problems with the people here – that we were all too polite to say anything to them. But they soon learnt differently. After a few days, they no longer did their food shopping at the supermarket. Michael Reed went away for two weeks and probably hoped everything would be forgotten when he got back."
"And what about the other two? Did they go away?" Frank holds his cup out for another cup of tea.
"No, they stayed here, although – as I said – no one really saw them

in the village afterwards. You know, I rather hoped it was their guilty *conscience* that made them die. Don't you think that is possible, Detective Durham?"

"It might be, Mrs Hutchinson. But I believe someone poisoned the three men."

"Poisoned?" Mrs Hutchinson *gasps*. "How horrible! Do you have any idea who the murderer is?"

"I'm not really allowed to talk about our *investigation* with you, Mrs Hutchinson." Frank *grins* and *shrugs his shoulders*. "Almost everyone in the village seems to have a good motive, except you, of course, Mrs Hutchinson!"

"Well, I'm VERY glad to hear it," says Mrs Hutchinson.

Ten minutes later, on their way back to Norwich in the car, Frank hits Barry playfully on the arm. "So, shall we go back for chocolate cake tomorrow? I'm sure Mrs Hutchinson would like to see you!"

Barry *grimaces*. "She *reminds me of* my history teacher. She *used to* look at me like that, too!"

At 10 a.m. the following morning, Frank and Barry are standing in front of Michael Reed's house when they see Mrs Hutchinson on the other side of the street. She *waves* and starts to cross the road.

"Good morning, you two. Have you got the keys for Mr Reed's house? Are you going to see if the murderer left any *clues*? Should I come in with you? I'm very good at finding *clues*, you know."

"That's very kind of you, Mrs Hutchinson, but I think it would be better if we worked on our own," answers Frank in a serious voice. "We can't let people say you *solved* the crime for us, can we?"

Mrs Hutchinson smiles. "I understand," she says. "But you will still be coming over later for tea, I hope."

Before either Frank or Barry can think of an excuse, Mrs Hutchinson turns and walks away.

"Oh great," *mutters* Frank. "We'll have to phone her later."
Barry *shrugs his shoulders*.
"We'd better go in, then, before anyone else invites us to tea." Frank turns the key in the lock and walks into the empty house.
There is a lot of post on the floor from the last few days and there is an even bigger *pile* of post on the table next to the door.
"One way not to pay your bills," Barry remarks.
They walk into the *lounge*. On the small coffee table is a TV magazine.
Frank looks at the date of the magazine. "This magazine is over four weeks old. Michael Reed probably bought it when he got back from his two-week trip away."
"That's a bit strange," *comments* Barry. "It is a weekly magazine, isn't it?"
"Yes."
In the kitchen there is a strong smell of bad food. Barry opens the fridge and quickly closes it again. "Yuk, that fridge is alive."
Frank is *puzzled*. "He only died three days ago. The things in the fridge are much older. There is a *pile* of unopened post and a TV magazine that is four weeks old. I don't think Mr Reed was here between the time he got back from his trip and his death. So where was he?"
"But PC Jones says he found him here."
"Can you give him a call and ask him to come over for a few minutes? I think he lives in this street. I'll have a look upstairs." Frank walks upstairs and into the bedroom. There is a suit on the *wardrobe* door. He puts his hands into the pocket and finds two tickets for a concert that took place three weeks ago. Next door, in the room Mr Reed *obviously* used as an office, Frank sees an answering machine. The tape is full. He presses the *rewind button* and listens to the messages. They are all over three weeks old.

He hears Barry open the door for PC Jones, so he walks downstairs, still *puzzled*.

Übung 12: Wie lautet der korrekte „question tag“?

ÜBUNG 12

1. He reads a TV magazine, *doesn't he?*

2. He is an investment expert, ____________?

3. Detective Durham knows Mrs Hutchinson, ____________?

4. Michael Reed got back from his trip two weeks ago, __________?

5. Mr Monks will find a job soon, ____________?

6. That would be nice, ____________?

"Where exactly did you find Mr Reed, *Constable*?" asks Frank.
"In his bed. Smelt and looked awful." The *constable* shudders.
"What did he have on?"
"Some pyjamas. Really dirty they were, too."
"Did you find the other men, too?"
"Yes."
"What did they have on?"
"They were in pyjamas, too."
"What made you go to the houses each time?"
PC Jones thinks for a minute. "Miss Chambers told me about Nicholas Fields. She told me she went round to his house to get something back that belonged to her. When he didn't answer the *bell* or her calls, she decided to ask me to go round and check."
Frank *scratches* the back of his ear. "And Mr Edmonton?"
Again PC Jones pauses while he thinks. "That was Mr Monks. He

said he couldn't get through to Mr Edmonton and was worried he might be hurt. And he also told me about Mr Reed."

"There is something VERY *suspicious* about those two," *comments* Frank, after the policeman has left.

"Yes," agrees Barry.

"Miss Chambers told us that Nicholas Fields sent her all her stuff back soon after she left the job at the architects. And I ran through Mr Reed's tape on the answering machine when I was upstairs and I didn't hear one message from Mr Monks."

"Time to go and see them again..." Barry pulls on his jacket.

"This time with a *search warrant*," *mutters* Frank *grimly*.

As they leave the house, they see Mrs Hutchinson outside. She is speaking to PC Jones. She smiles at the *constable* when he says goodbye, but when she turns round she looks very worried. She *leans* on her stick and walks over to speak to Frank and Barry.

Frank *frowns*. "Yes, Mrs Hutchinson, what is it?"

"I have found out something about Mr Monks and Miss Chambers that I think you should know," she says, almost in a whisper.

"Ah?" Frank's anger disappears immediately. "What is it?"

"I can't tell you here, you will have to come with me."

"One of us is going to have to go and pick up two *search warrants* at some point..." Frank looks hopefully at Barry who *nods*.

"Oh, but you'll come for a cup of tea first, won't you?" Mrs Hutchinson *insists*. "It is so important. I have bought a cake specially for you."

Better *humour* the woman, thinks Frank. It would be sad if she decided not to tell us what she knows.

Again the two detectives follow the tiny old lady into her house and then into the dining room. She goes out into the kitchen and comes back after five minutes with the silver *tray*, three cups and saucers, and a big chocolate cake.

"So what can you tell us, Mrs Hutchinson?" Frank asks as he takes a cup of tea from her. He doesn't want Mr Monks or Miss Chambers to have a *chance* to escape.
"I've got the thing over here," Mrs Hutchinson says and walks over to a drawer and takes out an *envelope*. She brings it back to the table and sits down. With a little smile, she picks up her cup of tea and takes a sip. "Exciting, isn't it?" she giggles.
Barry looks at her and smiles. Somehow he likes this funny woman with her *old-fashioned manners*. She makes such a nice change from the *bad-tempered* people in the town. He takes another bite of the chocolate cake and begins to feel very relaxed.
Frank, on the other hand, begins to feel impatient. They are wasting time. He sees Mrs Hutchinson watching him. She *sniffs* and looks a bit unhappy.
"Don't you like my tea and cake, Detective Durham?"
Frank sighs. "I am not a great cake fan, Mrs Hutchinson, but the tea is great."
To prove it, he *swallows* the rest of his tea and pushes his cup towards the teapot to show he wants another cup. Mrs Hutchinson smiles happily.
"That's a good boy. Now I'll show you what I have in this *envelope*," she says and pulls out two X-rays and a letter from a doctor.
"What have these got to do with the murder?" Frank asks *puzzled*.
"Oh, nothing at all," answers Mrs Hutchinson *brightly*. "But they are important for Miss Chambers and Mr Monks."
"I don't understand." Frank looks over at Barry to see if he has missed something, but sees that Barry is not really listening. He is holding his cake fork in one hand and *is staring* out of the window.
"Barry? Are you all right?"
Barry turns to Frank with a slightly *dazed expression*. "Sorry. I was sure I just saw Mr Monks and Miss Chambers at the window."

"Ah, perfect timing, as ever!" Mrs Hutchinson stands up. "Now you just sit there while I let them in. You can read this letter."
She puts the letter in front of Frank so he can read it easily. She *tuts* as she sees Barry still has the cake fork in his hand. "Let me put that down for you," she says and takes it out of his hand.
"This is all a bit *weird*," *mutters* Frank. He reads the letter. "This is from the hospital in Norwich. Mrs Hutchinson went there for tests last month. She has *cancer* and this letter says there is nothing that the doctors can do about it."
"I'm not feeling very well," *mutters* Barry suddenly.
Frank sees that a white liquid is coming out of Barry's mouth.
Frank tries to stand up, but his legs don't seem to want to move. He looks at the tea and cake and realizes what has happened. *Poison*! He panics. Perhaps there is still a *chance*. He reaches very slowly into his pocket and manages to get his mobile phone. He presses 9-9-9 and slowly lifts the phone to his ear. He hears the number beginning to ring, but before someone answers, a man's hand takes the phone out of his hand. Frank tries to turn his head to see who it is, but can't.

ÜBUNG 13 !

Übung 13: Welcher Satz enthält die korrekte Übersetzung?

1. Sie gibt ihm das Schreiben.
   a) ☐ She gives him the letter.
   b) ☐ She gives to him the letter.

2. Ich habe gestern einen Kuchen für Sie gebacken.
   a) ☐ I baked yesterday a cake for you.
   b) ☐ I baked a cake for you yesterday.

3. Sie erinnert Barry an sein Versprechen.
   a) ☐ She remembers Barry of his promise.
   b) ☐ She reminds Barry of his promise.

4. Frank und Barry folgen der Frau ins Esszimmer.
   a) ☐ Frank and Barry follow the woman into the dining room.
   b) ☐ Frank and Barry follow the woman into the dinner room.

5. Barry fühlt sich nicht gut.
   a) ☐ Barry doesn't feel good.
   b) ☐ Barry doesn't feel well.

Mrs Hutchinson comes back into view. She looks at Frank sympathetically and *gently strokes* his hand. "Now, now Detective Durham, we can't let you phone the police."
"I don't understand..." Frank *mutters*.
"Sit down for a moment, you two," Mrs Hutchinson says. "He has a right to know. It is going to take about another fifteen minutes *anyway*, after I drink my tea."
Frank watches as Mrs Hutchinson *pours* herself a large cup of tea from the pot.
"Now, you know what to do, don't you?" she asks and looks at the two people who are sitting next to Frank. "In a few minutes I will not be able to help you any more."
"Yes, of course, Mrs Hutchinson."
"We will do everything exactly the way you told us, Mrs Hutchinson."
The voices belong to Miss Chambers and Mr Monks, Frank is sure, but he can't turn his head to see them.
"Good." Mrs Hutchinson picks up her cup and drinks the tea. When she finishes it, she gives a little sigh and turns back to look at

Frank. "It is all rather tragic really," she remarks and *strokes* Frank's hand again. "It was such a nice neighbourhood here until those horrible men came to live here. There was no way that I could let the three of them get away with such bad behaviour. I have a big cellar here. It was perfect. There are no windows, so nobody can hear people inside. We put Mr Fields, Mr Edmonton and, later, Mr Reed down there and put rat *poison* in their drinks. Just a little at a time. We wanted them to be sorry, you see. They had been SO naughty!"

Mrs Hutchinson tidies her scarf and looks down the table at Barry, who looks as if he *is asleep*.

Mrs Hutchinson starts to fall forward. "Could you help me a bit, dears?" she asks.

Mr Monks and Miss Chambers come into view and carefully help Mrs Hutchinson back into the chair.

"Thank you," Mrs Hutchinson *mutters* and looks back at Frank. "*Anyway*, to cut a long story short, we thought it would not be difficult to make it look as if I did the murders on my own. I am dying *anyway*, as you see from that letter. I have written a letter to say that I gave the men rat *poison* and put it with my *will* at the *mayor's* office. It's a *shame* the *mayor* listened to Dr Sterling."

Mrs Hutchinson sighs. "PC Jones, *bless him*, is not a problem, but I knew you would soon guess that the men did not die at home – and that is a problem. I can't allow anything else to happen to my two friends. So that, *I'm afraid*, is why we had to change our plans. Mr Monks has already phoned your police station to say that you are on the way to the station with me because I have *confessed* to the murders."

Frank looks at Mrs Hutchinson and tries to say something.

The old lady understands his question and shakes her head. "Oh no, they won't find the *poison* in your stomach, Detective Durham.

Unfortunately, on the way to the police station, we will have a *nasty* car accident... on that bend between Southfield and Millwood. It is such a dangerous corner. Cars often *skid* off the road there. They *catch fire* and burn completely – and it is very difficult to identify the car after such an accident. There is never much left of the *bodies*... teeth, perhaps. But certainly nothing much for the *pathologists*..."

This is *madness*, Frank thinks. He is now finding it almost impossible to keep his eyes open. Mrs Hutchinson smiles at him weakly. Then she slowly looks at Miss Chambers, who is putting the tea things on the *tray*.

"I think you can take Detective Durham's keys now, dear. He's almost gone. And by the time you bring the car back, we'll all be ready."

MURDER IN BATTERSEA PARK

Bernie Martin

Chapter 1: The Murder

It's 6 a.m. and *Constable* Andrew Parker is jogging. Jogging is his hobby, and he runs through Battersea Park in London, which is just a couple of miles south of Marble Arch. He runs four days a week and likes to look at the black swans on the lake. As he jogs past the playing area, he notices a young girl who is sitting on a bench with her head in her hands. He calls out and asks if she's okay, and she smiles at him and answers that she's just a bit tired. Satisfied, Andrew Parker jogs on to the end of the park where he turns round and runs back the way he has come.

A few minutes later, as he is about to pass the bench on his way back, he sees the girl still sitting there. She is now *leaning* back on the bench and seems to *be asleep*. Andrew Parker sees that her handbag has fallen to the ground. He smiles, jogs over and picks it up. As he puts the bag next to her on the bench, the girl's head falls to one side. Andrew puts his hands out to stop her from hurting herself. His hands *support* the back of her head, but she is getting heavier. He *gently* rests her head on the bench and feels that something is terribly wrong.

"Miss? Are you okay? Miss?"

She doesn't reply. Andrew realizes that the girl *isn't asleep*. He lets go of her head and starts to reach for her bag to find out who she is, when he realizes that his hands are wet and *sticky*. He looks in horror at the blood on his hands. He feels for a pulse, but there isn't one. He checks his watch, it's 6:14 a.m., then he takes out his mobile phone and calls his colleagues.

At twenty past six, Detective Inspector Robert Kenny *is fast asleep* and *snoring*. He suddenly hears a *bell* ringing and reaches to the bedside table to switch the alarm clock off. His fingers find the button of the alarm clock, but the *bell* continues ringing. He hears his wife's voice *mumbling* in the dark.

"It's the telephone."

More awake now, he reaches over and lifts the *receiver*.

"Hello?"

"Inspector Kenny?"

"Yes. Do you know what time it is?"

"Yes. Sorry, Inspector, but we have a murder."

Inspector Kenny wakes up very quickly. "Where?"

"In Battersea Park, sir."

"When?"

"About fifteen minutes ago. It was actually a *constable* who discovered the *body* while he was jogging. He's still there now."

"Right. I'm on my way. Can you inform Sergeant North?"

"That's next on my list, Inspector."

"Tell her to meet me in the park."

"I'll do that. Goodbye, Inspector."

Robert Kenny jumps out of bed and goes for a quick shower. As he is getting dressed, his wife Judith looks at him with sleepy eyes.

"Don't forget."

"What, Judith?"

"We are going to Alfredo's for our *wedding anniversary* at 7 p.m. this evening."

"Yes. Right. Of course."

Judith sits up in bed.

"You forgot, didn't you?"

"Of course not!"

Robert Kenny goes to the bed and gives Judith a kiss on the cheek.

As he closes the bedroom door behind him, he lets out a deep sigh. "Thank God she *reminded me*!"

Übung 1: Enträtseln Sie die folgenden Definitionen!

1. Running to stay fit. __________ (gonggij)
2. You sit on this in a park. __________ (hebnc)
3. Ladies put their things in this. __________ (bangadh)
4. Feel this to see if someone's alive. __________ (slupe)
5. Making a noise when asleep. __________ (rones)
6. Standing under water to wash. __________ (roshew)
7. Celebrate your wedding day. __________ (revaniransy)

Battersea Park isn't far from Inspector Kenny's home and he arrives there at ten to seven. Two colleagues are keeping back the curious people behind tape which is protecting the scene of the crime. Dr Jenkins, the police *pathologist*, is bent down and examining the *body*. Inspector Kenny goes to him and says good morning.

"Good morning, Inspector."

"Can you tell me anything yet, Dr Jenkins?"

"It was definitely murder. She was hit on the back of the head with a heavy object."

Inspector Kenny bends down to get a closer look.

"She looks very young."

"She's nineteen years old, *according to* her student's card. She died between six and six fifteen."

"How can you be so accurate? I hear that you are very good, Doctor, but you must be a genius."

The doctor laughs.

"Actually, Inspector, I'm not a genius. It's all thanks to your colleague."

"You mean the person who found the *body*?"

"Exactly. *Constable* Parker. He passed her at about 6 a.m. and when he came back at about six fifteen, she was dead."

"Is he still here?"

"Yes. That's him over there, in the jogging suit standing under the large tree."

"Do you remember the name on the student's card, Doctor?"

"Yes. It's Linda Farraday. Your office is already checking on it."

"Great. Thanks very much."

"You're welcome, Inspector."

Inspector Kenny stands up and brushes the earth from the knee of his trousers. He walks across to *Constable* Parker, who is still standing under the tree *muttering* to himself.

"Are you *Constable* Parker?"

"Yes, I am. I saw you talking to the doctor. Are you *in charge of* the *investigation*?"

"That's right. My name's Inspector Robert Kenny. Now, tell me exactly what happened."

At that moment, Sergeant Kelly North, Inspector Kenny's assistant, arrives.

"Good morning, Inspector. Good morning, sir," she says, looking at Parker in his jogging clothes.

"Good morning, Sergeant. Could you take notes, please?"

"Certainly, Inspector."

"Sergeant, this is *Constable* Albert Parker..."

"Excuse me, sir. It's Andrew Parker."

"I'm sorry. This is *Constable* Andrew Parker. He's our main *witness* in this *case*. Now, *Constable* Parker, please tell us exactly what happened this morning."

Constable Parker tells them what happened. Kelly North looks him up and down. She likes what she sees.

"*Constable* Parker? It seems strange that there was nobody in the park, even at 6 a.m."

"Well... When I was picking up the girl's handbag, I heard a noise behind the bushes. I looked up and saw a man running away."

Inspector Kenny looks up in interest.

"Can you describe him?"

"Yes, Inspector. He is quite tall and slim, about twenty-five years old. He has short dark hair and I seem to remember a silver *stud* in his left ear."

"That might help. Well done, *Constable*."

"Did you see anybody else?"

"Well, actually, there was a lady who was walking her dog, but she was a long way away."

Inspector Kenny walks away, mobile phone to his ear, to call his station with the description. Kelly North looks at Parker with interest.

"Ever thought of joining the C.I.D.?"

"The Criminal *Investigation* Department is my dream, Sergeant."

"Well, why don't you fill in an *application* and send it to me?"

"I'll do that, Sergeant. Thank you very much."

"*Don't mention it, Constable*."

Sergeant Kelly North walks away with a smile on her face. She goes over to Inspector Kenny, who is ready to leave.

"What were you talking to Parker about?"

"Oh, nothing, Sir. Just small talk."

"Right. We need to go and see the girl's family."

Kelly's smile disappears. She *nods grimly*.
"Right, Inspector."

Übung 2: Welches Wort ist das „schwarze Schaf"? Unterstreichen Sie das nicht in die Reihe passende Wort!

ÜBUNG 2

1. flat, house, apartment, home
2. protect, hit, bang, strike
3. walk, jog, run, swim
4. mother, father, young, aunt
5. tree, flower, bench, cactus
6. jeans, shirt, pullover, clothes
7. cat, tiger, dog, lion

They drive to the address and find that it is a big house in a very expensive part of Chelsea. They go to the front door and it is answered by a *middle-aged* woman. Inspector Kenny gives a little cough and gets ready to give the bad news.
"Mrs Farraday?"
"No, I'm Miss Dunbar, the *housekeeper*. How can I help you?"
"My name's Inspector Kenny and this is Sergeant North. We would like to speak to Mr and Mrs Farraday, please."
"That is not possible, *I'm afraid*."
"Why not?"
"Mrs Farraday died two years ago."
"I'm very sorry to hear that. Could we possibly speak to Mr Farraday?"
"Well, he's just about to leave for work."
"Miss Dunbar. This *matter* is very urgent. We're investigating a murder and we need to speak to Mr Farraday."

"Oh! In that *case*, you had better come in."

She *shows them into* a very large living room that is filled with *bookshelves* and *Chippendale furniture*. Miss Dunbar leaves to get Mr Farraday. The officers sit down, very carefully, on the chairs and wait.

A few minutes later, Mr Farraday enters the room. He is a tall, elegant *middle-aged* man and is dressed in a *pin-striped suit*.

"Good morning. You must be the people from the police. I hope it's not a problem with one of my patients?"

Inspector Kenny looks *confused*.

"Patients?"

"Yes. You see, I'm a doctor. My *surgery* is in Harley Street. I treat a lot of famous people and have many rock stars as patients."

"Now I see, Doctor. No, it's not one of your patients. It's your daughter, Linda."

"What is it this time? That girl is always getting into trouble. Have you *arrested* her?"

Inspector Kenny looks at the floor, and Kelly North *pretends* to be busy with her notes.

"*I'm afraid* I have some bad news for you, sir."

"Don't say it's drugs?"

"No, sir. Your daughter was murdered."

Dr Farraday shouts.

"Nooooo!"

Suddenly the door opens and a young girl comes running into the room. She *hugs* Dr Farraday.

"Daddy, what's wrong?"

"It's Linda. These people are saying she was murdered."

The girl looks at Kelly North with a question in her eyes. Kelly North *nods* and the girl *bursts into tears*.

"Oh! No! It can't be true!"

She *hugs* her father harder, and they both cry into each other's shoulders.
After a few minutes, Dr Farraday looks at Kenny and North.
"This is my daughter, Mandy. She is Linda's younger sister. What happened?"
Kelly North stands up.
"She was killed in Battersea Park. I'm sorry, sir... I know this isn't the right moment, but we have to get a positive identification of the *body* as soon as possible. Could you and Mandy come with us to the *morgue*?"
"What? You want us to identify the *body*?"
"You can do it, sir. Mandy doesn't have to."
"Yes, all right. I need to call my receptionist and cancel some appointments."
"That's fine, sir. We would also like to ask you both some questions at the station, after the *morgue*."
"Yes. I'll tell her to cancel all my appointments for today."
"What about my school, dad?"
"Yes, Mandy. Tell Miss Dunbar to ring them."

Chapter 2: The Questioning Begins

Übung 3: Lesen Sie weiter und unterstreichen Sie die Übersetzung der Wörter in Klammern!
(1. Tochter, 2. Tasse, 3. Nacht, 4. Streit, 5. adoptieren, 6. Ehefrau, 7. schwanger)

ÜBUNG 3 !

They drive to the *morgue*, where Dr Farraday identifies his daughter Linda. Then they drive to the police station and get a cup of tea. Inspector Kenny takes Dr Farraday into an interview room.

"Dr Farraday. First let me apologize for putting you through all this."
"I know that you are just doing your job, Inspector."
"When was the last time you saw Linda, Dr Farraday?"
"Last night. She was leaving for her job at the disco."
"Do you know the name of the disco, sir?"
"Yes. It's the Starlight."
"What time was this?"
"About 9 p.m."
"Did she seem normal?"
"Normal! What's normal for a nineteen-year-old teenager?"
"So she wasn't acting normally?"
"Actually, we had a little *argument*."
"What was it about, sir?"
"The same as always. Linda broke off her *medical studies* and was working in that disco. She changed so much when her mother died."
"Yes. I'm sorry to hear that, sir."
"Well, actually, Susan wasn't her real mother. We tried for years to have children, but couldn't. Then we decided to *adopt*. Linda was only a baby when we got her."
"So Mandy is adopted too, sir?"
"Actually, no. We had Linda for about a year, then my wife Susan became pregnant."
"I see."

"To get back to last night, sir. So Linda left the house *upset*?"
"Well, not really. We agreed that Linda would give up her job at the disco and that she would continue her *medical studies* in New Zealand next month."
"So everything was *settled* then?"
"Yes. At least I thought it was," Dr Farraday replies.

In another room, Kelly North is interviewing Mandy Farraday.
"When was the last time you saw your sister, Mandy?"
"Yesterday evening as she was leaving for work."
"Did Linda seem *upset* or worried?"
"No. Linda loved her job at the disco."
"Where did she work?"
"The Starlight Disco."
"So, how did you *get on with* your sister?"
"We *got on* well. I mean we fought sometimes, but I don't know any sisters that don't."
"Yes, of course. I must say, you and Linda didn't look like sisters."
"That's because we weren't. Linda was adopted, you know?"
"I didn't know that."
"Oh yes. I'm daddy's only real child. I'm going to study medicine and become a doctor like him. He'll be so *proud* of me."
"Mandy, can you think of anyone who would want to kill your sister?"
"No. Everyone loved Linda. She was always the *centre of attention*."
"Do you have any idea why Linda was in Battersea Park at six in the morning?"
"She usually finished work at about 4 a.m. I suppose she went to the park for some fresh air before going home."
"Well. That's about all for now. I'll call you if I need to speak to you again."
Back in their office, Inspector Kenny looks at the clock on the wall and sees that it's nearly half past twelve.
"Let's go to the canteen for lunch, Kelly."
"Good idea, Robert. I'm *starving*."
Kenny and North discuss the *case* over lunch. They decide to visit the Starlight Disco that afternoon.

ÜBUNG 4 !

Übung 4: Fügen Sie die Übersetzung der angegebenen Wörter ein!

When they arrive there the disco is (1. leer) __________, but there is a young (2. Frau) __________ behind the bar, who is polishing glasses. She is about twenty-five years old, rather *plump* and she is wearing too much make-up.

"Sorry. We don't (3. aufmachen) __________ until this evening."

North and Kenny take out and (4. zeigen) __________ their *identity cards*.

"Oh! You're the police. I suppose you've come to (5. fragen) __________ about Linda?"

Kelly North takes out her (6. Notizbuch) __________.

"That's right. How do you know about Linda? The information hasn't been *released* to the press yet."

"Dr Farraday (7. angerufen) __________ about half an hour ago, to tell us that Linda was killed this morning."

(8. Tränen) __________ fill her eyes and she takes a *tissue* out of her handbag.

"We *got on* really well, you know."
"Could you give me your name, please?"
"Oh! Sure, sorry. I'm Sandra Williams. Linda and I worked together most of the time," the woman answers.

"When was the last time you saw Linda, Ms Williams?"
"This morning. We did the *late shift* and finished just after five in the morning."
"Did you leave together?"
"No. Linda said she needed to talk to Ned. She seemed very excited about something."
"Do you know what she was excited about?"
"No, I'm sorry. I don't. I did ask, but she said she'd tell me this evening."
Inspector Kenny is busy studying the photographs of the table dancers. Suddenly a door at the back of the disco opens and a tall man enters.
"What's going on here? *I'm afraid* I must ask you to leave."
Inspector Kenny walks across the room to him. He remembers *Constable* Parker's description.
"He is tall, slim with short dark hair, wearing a silver *stud* in his left ear."
The description *matches* perfectly. Inspector Kenny shows him his *identity card.*
"Inspector Kenny, C.I.D."
The man *backs off* a step.
"Police, here in my club. What do you want?"
Kenny continues.
"Let me *clear something up*. I'm the one who asks the questions. Have you got that?"
"Yes, officer."
"Now. Who are you and what are you doing here?"
"My name's Ned Taylor and I'm the owner of this club."
"Very good, Mr Taylor. You learn fast. I think you heard about Linda Farraday, didn't you?"
"Yes, of course. Terrible thing," Mr Taylor replies.

"Mr Taylor. Where were you at 6 a.m. this morning?"
"I was at home. I was getting ready for bed."
"Are you sure, Mr Taylor?"
"Of course I'm sure."
"Mr Ned Taylor, I'm *arresting* you on *suspicion* of murdering Linda Farraday!"
Ned Taylor and Sandra Williams look up in shock as Inspector Kenny closes the *handcuffs* on Taylor's wrists. He looks across at Sandra Williams.
"Ms Williams. I would like you to come to the station, too. We have more questions for you."
Sandra Williams *hesitates*.
"What about the club?"
Ned Taylor *waves* his handcuffed hands at her.
"Sandra, just lock up and come with us. Okay?"
"If you say so, Ned."
She gets her handbag and as they leave the club, she locks up behind her.

ÜBUNG 5 !

Übung 5: Beantworten Sie folgende Fragen zum Text!

1. Where was Mr Taylor at 6 a.m. this morning?

___

2. What is the name of Inspector Kenny's assistant?

___

3. What is the name of the murdered girl?

___

4. What is the name of Mr Taylor's disco?

____

5. What is the name of the woman who worked with Linda?

____

6. What does Mr Taylor wear in his left ear?

____

When they arrive at the station, they hand Ned Taylor over to the *duty sergeant*, who puts him in a cell. Another officer takes Sandra Williams to an interview room. Kelly North gets her a cup of tea and biscuits and tells her that she will be back very soon. She then goes to Inspector Kenny's office.

"There you are, Kelly. What do you think?"

"You shocked me when you *arrested* Taylor, Robert."

"Why? You know *Constable* Parker saw someone who fits his description in the park this morning."

"It just seems too easy. Maybe he wasn't the only one in the park."

"You could be right, Kelly. I'm hoping that by putting Ned Taylor in a cell, he will be *scared* enough to tell the truth."

"Good idea, Robert."

"Look. Let's *interrogate* Williams together first. You might hear something I don't. After that we'll do Taylor."

"Okay, you're the boss."

They go to the interview room where Sandra Williams is waiting for them.

They sit down opposite her, and Inspector Kenny starts the interrogation.

"Right, Ms Williams. You told Sergeant North that you last saw Linda Farraday just after five this morning. Is that correct?"

"Yes, that's right, Inspector," Sandra Williams replies.

"How was your working relationship with Ms Farraday?"

"Very good."

"What about your boss, Ned Taylor?"

"Well. He's a difficult man to work for, but very fair. Of course, Linda *got on with* him better than I did."

"Why do you say that?"

"Don't you know? They were lovers!"

Inspector Kenny and Sergeant North look at each other in surprise.

"Do you know her family?"

"Well, I met Dr Farraday once. A real gentleman."

"What about her sister?"

"You mean Mandy. Oh yes, I know her. I don't think that she's a very nice person."

"So you don't like her?"

"Nobody I know does. Especially Linda."

"Why?"

"She was always *reminding* Linda that she was adopted. She was often telling lies about Linda, trying to get her into trouble," Sandra Williams answers.

"So Linda and Mandy didn't *get on,* then?"

"Not at all. Linda only tried to *get on with* Mandy because of her father. She was looking forward to going to New Zealand."

"One last question, Ms Willams. Do you think Ned Taylor could have killed Linda?"

Sandra Williams looks shocked.

"No. I don't think so. He always plays the hard man, but I don't think he would kill someone."

"Well, thank you very much, Ms Williams. You were a big help."

"Should I go and open the club now?"

"Yes, if you wish. Goodbye."

Übung 6: Unterstreichen Sie die zehn Wörter, die falsch geschrieben sind, und verbessern Sie sie!

Robert Kenny and Kelly North take her to the door and ask the *duty sergeant* to brought Ned Taylor to hte interview room.
"Kelly, wen we *interrogate* Taylor, do you want to be the good guy or the baad guy?"
"Let me be the good guy *for a change*. You playt the good guy last week."
"Okay, here he come."
Ned Taylor is led in and sits on the chair opposite thems. Kelly North smiles at him.
"Mr Taylor. Would you like a kup of tea?"
Robert Kenny interrupts rudely.
"No tea for the prisoner, Sergeant!"
"Fery well, Inspector. Now, Mr Taylor, do you have ani *objection* to us recording this interview?"

1. ______________________
2. ______________________
3. ______________________
4. ______________________
5. ______________________
6. ______________________
7. ______________________
8. ______________________
9. ______________________
10. ______________________

"No." Mr Taylor is *obviously* nervous.
"Could you please *state* your full name for the record?"
"Edward Nigel Taylor."
"But you're known as 'Ned', aren't you?"
"Yes, that's right," Taylor replies nervously.

"Please *state* your address, Mr Taylor."
"It's 31 Highbury Road, Chelsea."
Robert Kenny *leans* over angrily.
"Don't *mess us about*, Sonny. Give us the postcode as well."
Taylor looks *scared*.
"Er, sorry. It's SW6 1HS."
Kelly North smiles sweetly.
"Thank you very much, Mr Taylor."
"You're welcome, Officer."
There's a knock at the door and *Constable* Parker enters, carrying a *tray*. He gives Ned Taylor a cup and looks *intently* at his face. Ned Taylor is *obviously* uncomfortable.
"Tell him to stop *staring* at me."
Constable Parker walks round the table and puts a cup of tea in front of Inspector Kenny. As he does this he *whispers* in his ear.
"It's him, Inspector. One hundred per cent."
"Thank you, *Constable*. You may leave now."
Kelly North shakes her head in amused surprise. Robert Kenny continues to play the bad guy.

ÜBUNG 7 !

Übung 7: Ordnen Sie die Wörter auf der rechten Seite den Begriffen auf der linken zu!

1. ☐ state	a) bang, strike, hit
2. ☐ nervous	b) mug, pot, glass
3. ☐ scared	c) go, depart, exit
4. ☐ cup	d) say, report, inform
5. ☐ stop	e) halt, cease, finish
6. ☐ knock	f) afraid, terrified, fearful
7. ☐ leave	g) worried, anxious, upset

"So, Ned, why did you kill Linda Farraday?"
"What!" He jumps to his feet.
"I didn't kill her."
Inspector Kenny *leans* over the table and pushes Ned back onto the chair. Kelly North shakes her head.
"Sir, I must protest..."
Inspector Kenny turns to her and *winks* but shouts angrily, "Sergeant North! I am your direct *superior*. Take your notes, but *let me handle this*."
Kelly North *pretends* to be *upset*.
"Yes, sir."
"Now then, Taylor. Why did you lie to me?"
"What! When? I mean."
"In your club you told me that you were at home at six this morning. Before you lie again, we have a *witness* who saw you in Battersea Park at that time."
"Well, your *witness* must be lying."
"Mr Taylor. Our *witness* is a policeman. I am giving you one last *chance*. Either you tell us everything, or I will put you back in the cell and throw away the key."
Ned Taylor hangs his head *in defeat*.
"Okay. I admit I lied."
"So why don't you tell the truth *for a change*?"
"Yes, I was in the park at six this morning. When she was finishing work, Linda told me that she was expecting my baby."
"How did you react?"
"Badly, *I'm afraid*. I was shocked. *Anyway*, we started to have an *argument*, but Linda was *scared* Sandra would hear."
"So you arranged to meet in the park?"
"Yes. We often went there after work to *come down a bit*."
"What happened exactly, Mr Taylor?"

"I was a bit late. I saw a woman walking a dog and a jogger who was running in the other *direction*. I came round the corner and walked to the bench from behind."
"Why from behind?"
"Well, it was one of our games. I would *cover* her eyes with my hands and Linda would have to guess who it was."
"I see. So did she guess it was you?"
"No. I got to within a few *yards* and saw that she was half lying on the bench. Then I saw the blood on the back of her head and panicked."
"So you ran away?"
"I'm not *proud* of it, but yes. I saw the jogger coming back and knew that I would get *blamed for* the murder, so I ran."
"Are you sure you are telling the truth?"
"I swear, Inspector. I loved Linda. I was going to ask her to marry me. She was expecting my child!"
"Right, Mr Taylor. *That's all for now. I'm afraid* you have to go back to your cell for the time being."
"Anything you say, Inspector. Honestly, I am not the murderer."
Inspector Kenny rings for an *escort,* and a *constable* takes Ned Taylor back to his cell. Kenny turns to Sergeant North.
"So, Kelly. What do you think?"
"Well. It certainly looks as though Ned Taylor is the killer. What can his motive be?" the sergeant replies.
"I don't know. Maybe he didn't want to marry her. I'm sure that will become clear soon enough."
"I don't know, Robert. It all seems too easy."
"What do you mean?" the inspector asks.
"Well. Ned Taylor in the park. I think it could be any of them. Dr Farraday, Mandy, or even Sandra Williams."
"What motive could her father have?"

"Dr Farraday is a very conservative man. The *shame* was too much for him, perhaps," Sergeant North replies.
"What about Mandy Farraday? Surely you don't think it was her?"
"Maybe!"
"But she's only seventeen," Inspector Kenny *states*.
"You heard what Sandra Williams said about Mandy and Linda not liking each other."
"So you think one of them is lying?"
"I do, and I'm *betting* it's Mandy."
"How about this, Kelly? Sandra Williams is in love with Ned Taylor. She *overhears* Linda telling Ned she is pregnant and wants him to marry her. She follows Linda to Battersea Park and kills her in a *jealous rage*?"
"Also possible, Robert. So, what do we do now?"
"What do you suggest, Kelly?"
"Maybe we should question them all again?"

Übung 8: Bringen Sie die Wörter in die richtige Reihenfolge!

1. the am I murderer not

2. woman saw I dog a walking a

3. my was she child expecting

4. be motive his what can ?

5. too seems easy it all

6. Ned in Sandra love with is

"You're right, Kelly. Let's question them all again tomorrow. I must run now. If I'm not on time for our anniversary dinner, my wife will kill me."

"Congratulations, Robert. Which one is it?"

Robert Kenny thinks for a while. He jumps when the telephone next to his elbow rings.

"Robert Kenny speaking?"

"Dr Jenkins here. We spoke at the *crime scene* in Battersea Park this morning."

"Yes, Doctor. Just let me switch you to the loudspeaker. My colleague should hear this, too. Okay, go ahead."

"Right. Linda Farraday died after *receiving* a *severe* blow to the back of the head. After you left, we found a heavy tree branch, in the bushes, behind the *body*. There was blood on it, so we took it to the laboratory with us. We tested it and discovered that it is definitely the murder weapon."

"Are there any fingerprints on the branch, Doctor?"

"*I'm afraid* not. Sorry."

"Thanks very much..."

"Oh, Inspector. There's one more thing."

"Yes, Doctor?"

"Linda Farraday was about ten weeks' pregnant."

"That's a big help. Thanks very much, Dr Jenkins. Goodbye."

Inspector Kenny hangs up and starts to put his jacket on.

"So, Robert. How many years have you been married?"

"You know, Kelly, I really can't say. Eleven, I think."
Kelly North smiles and reaches for her coat.

Chapter 3: Turning Up the Heat

The next morning they *interrogate* Dr Farraday first. Inspector Kenny greets him politely.
"Good morning, Dr Farraday. We are really sorry to *bother* you again."
"No problem. I know you're only doing your job. *Besides*, I want Linda's killer caught."
"Exactly. We only have a few questions for you, Doctor."
"Ask anything you like."
"Mandy told us yesterday that she and Linda *got on* well, but Sandra Williams says it was the opposite."
"Who is Sandra Williams?"
"She's Linda's colleague. They worked together at the Starlight disco."
"Oh, I see. Well, to be perfectly honest, I'm not too sure. You see, I work long hours and haven't seen too much of my girls recently. You'll have to ask Miss Dunbar, my *housekeeper*. She saw them more often than me."
"What's your feeling, Doctor? Did they *get on* well?"
"Of course they argued a lot, like most sisters. I sometimes had the feeling that Mandy was *jealous of* Linda."
"How do you mean?"
"Well. Little things, really. Mandy always *blamed* Linda if anything went wrong. Linda's favourite clothes would disappear and Miss Dunbar would find them in the back of Mandy's *wardrobe*. Of course, Mandy would say that Linda did it herself to get her into trouble," Dr Farraday sighs and shakes his head.

"Thank you, Dr Farraday. Now, one last question. Where were you at 6 a.m. yesterday morning?"

Dr Farraday gets *upset*.

"*How dare you*! Do you honestly think I killed my own daughter?"

"Adopted daughter, Dr Farraday."

"I *raised* that girl as my own. My wife, too. I loved her just as much as Mandy."

"Please just answer the question, Doctor."

"I was in bed. Where else would I be at six in the morning?"

"Thank you for your help, Doctor. *That's all for now.*"

ÜBUNG 9

Übung 9: Füllen Sie die Lücken der folgenden Sätze mit den Präpositionen ***on, at*** *oder* ***in****!*

1. The alarm rang early __________ the morning.
2. It was cold __________ the park.
3. Linda and Mandy didn't get __________ well.
4. Kelly met Robert __________ the station.
5. Dr Farraday works long hours __________ his surgery.
6. __________ 6 a.m., I was __________ bed.
7. They talked __________ the interview room.
8. I'll see you __________ Monday.

The next person to come in is Sandra Williams.

"Good morning, Ms Williams. Please take a seat."

She sits down and starts *fumbling* in her handbag. Kelly North *leans* over to her.

"What's the problem, Ms Williams? Are you looking for something?"

"No. Yes. I can't find my *tissues*."

"Here, use these."

Kelly stands up and gets a box of *tissues* from a sideboard.

"Oh, thank you, Miss. You are so kind."

"No problem, Ms Williams. Now then, we have a few more questions for you."

"Okay."

"You told us yesterday that Linda and Mandy didn't *get on*. Is this true?"

"Of course. Why should I lie? Linda just didn't make a big deal of it out of respect for her father."

"Do you think Mandy killed her sister?"

"Oh, my God. You can't believe...? No. I know Mandy hated Linda, but kill her...?"

"Hate is a very strong word, Ms Williams."

"Well, Mandy did hate her! Wouldn't you if your sister stole your boyfriend?"

Kelly North *leans* back in surprise.

"Could you say that again?"

"What? I thought you knew. When Linda started to work at the Starlight, Mandy came with her. *Anyway*, she fell in love with Ned and they started seeing each other."

"So what happened then?"

"Well, about six months ago, Ned finished with Mandy and started seeing Linda. There were explosions, I can tell you!"

"Did you have a relationship with Mr Taylor?"

"No. I mean, I *fancy* him, but he's not interested in me."

"Okay, Ms Williams. Oh, one more thing. Where were you at six yesterday morning?"

Sandra Williams starts crying.
"I went straight home from the club. No, wait. On my way home, I stopped at the bakery at the end of my street. I had to wait a few minutes, because they don't open until six."
"What's the name of the bakery and the street, Ms Williams?"
"Crofts. I think it's number 43, Henshall Avenue."
"Right. We will check that. Thank you very much, Ms Williams."

Robert Kenny looks in the phone book and calls the bakery while they are waiting for Ned Taylor. He speaks to the baker's wife and describes Sandra Williams. The baker's wife knows Sandra quite well and Inspector Kenny *receives confirmation* that Sandra Williams was there at six the day before. Ned Taylor enters the room still in *handcuffs*. The police *escort* sits him in the chair opposite North and Kenny, *nods* and leaves.
Inspector Kenny looks at Taylor for a long time without saying anything. Ned Taylor becomes more and more nervous. Finally, Robert Kenny *leans* back in his chair.
"Mr Taylor. Why didn't you tell us about Mandy yesterday?"
"Mandy Farraday? Well, I didn't think it was important."
"How about letting us decide what's important, Mr Taylor? Tell us about Mandy."
"Well. She sort of forced the relationship on me. She's young and I thought it would be good for my ego, you know?"
"No. I don't know, Mr Taylor."
"Sandra did warn me that Mandy only wanted to go out with me because Linda *fancied* me. I didn't believe her then, but now I'm not so sure."
"So you finished with Mandy to go out with Linda?"
"Not really. Mandy was always *demanding*. If she didn't get her way, she would *sulk*, as schoolgirls do."

"So you finished with her?" the inspector asks.

"Yes. I finished with her. She flew into a *rage* and accused me of *cheating on her* with Linda, but it wasn't like that. Linda and I didn't start seeing each other until a week later."

"So, Mandy accepted it in the end?"

"Not really. She *threatens* me constantly. She tried to get me in trouble with the *tax office* a few times and spread *nasty gossip* about me. About Linda, too, as far as I know."

"Do you think Mandy killed Linda?"

"No way! Mandy can be a little *minx* at times, but I can't believe she would kill her sister."

"Right, Mr Taylor. You can go home now."

"What? Really? I can go home?"

"Yes, but let us know where you are at all times. We might have to speak to you again."

"Yes, Inspector. I'll do that, and thanks."

Ned Taylor leaves the room very quickly.

Übung 10: Übersetzen Sie und enträtseln Sie das Lösungswort!

1. sicher _ _ □ _
2. sprechen _ _ _ □ _
3. wirklich □ _ _ _ _ _
4. Mädchen _ _ □ _
5. später _ □ _ _ _
6. entscheiden □ _ _ _ _ _
7. verlassen _ _ □ _ _
8. gestern □ _ _ _ _ _ _ _ _

Lösung: _ _ _ _ _ _ _ _

Chapter 4: The Killer Is Caught

Kelly North looks at Robert Kenny in surprise.
"Why are you letting him go, Robert?"
"Because he's not the killer."
"Well. Who is it then?"
"I'll tell you when I'm one hundred per cent sure," Inspector Kenny replies.
"Oh! I hate it when you do that."
"Kelly, *trust* me."
"Well there's only Mandy left to question now. Should I call her in, Inspector?"
"Not yet, Kelly. I want to make a quick phone call first," the inspector replies *thoughtfully*.
He takes Dr Farraday's business card out of his *wallet* and *dials* the number. He *covers* the mouthpiece and tells Sergeant North that he's putting the call on loudspeaker so that she can hear, too.
"Hello, Farraday residence. Miss Dunbar speaking?"
"Hello, Miss Dunbar. This is Inspector Kenny. We met yesterday."
"Yes, I remember, Inspector. What can I do for you?" the *housekeeper* asks.
"Well, Miss Dunbar. I'm just calling to confirm that Dr Farraday was in the house at 6 a.m. yesterday morning."
"He was, Inspector. He came down for breakfast at half past six, as always. He finished just before you arrived."
"I see. What about Mandy? What time does she usually have breakfast?"
"She usually comes down just after Dr Farraday."
"And yesterday?"
"Oh, she didn't have breakfast yesterday. She came home about ten minutes before you arrived."

"Are you sure, Miss Dunbar?" Inspector Kenny asks.
"Yes. You see, it was a full moon *the night before last* and I could not sleep. *Anyway*, I got up at about half past four to get a glass of water. Then I heard the front door closing and looked out of my bedroom window. That's when I saw Mandy walking towards town."
"Did she say where she went?"
"No, she didn't."
"Another question, Miss Dunbar. Did Mandy and Linda *get on with* each other?"
"They did before Mrs Farraday died. Then, Mandy changed. She was always telling Linda that she wasn't part of the family. Terrible thing, really."
"How was their relationship during the last few months?" Inspector Kenny asks.
"To be perfectly honest, Inspector, it went from bad to worse," the *housekeeper* sighs.
"Thank you, Miss Dunbar. That is a big help. Goodbye."
"Goodbye, Inspector."
Robert Kenny puts the phone down and turns to Kelly North.
"Mandy is the killer, Kelly. I'm sure of it."
"You could be right, Robert, but I think it was Ned Taylor."
"Yes, that's also possible. However, I can't see him killing his girlfriend because she was pregnant and wanted to marry him." Inspector Kenny shakes his head.
"Well, if it is Mandy, how do we prove it? We have no fingerprints on the branch, nobody believes that she could murder anyone, and nobody saw her at the scene of the crime."
"I have an idea. Call her in now."
Sergeant Kelly North opens the door and calls Mandy Farraday into the interview room.

ÜBUNG 11

Übung 11: Vervollständigen Sie die Aussagen!

1. When Kenny and North entered the disco, ______________.
   a) ☐ they were given a drink
   b) ☐ they were asked to leave
   c) ☐ Kenny banged his head

2. Battersea Park's lake has ______________.
   a) ☐ black swans
   b) ☐ white geese
   c) ☐ black ducks

3. Miss Dunbar got up to ______________.
   a) ☐ go to the bathroom
   b) ☐ get a glass of water
   c) ☐ get a cup of coffee

4. Linda wanted to study in ______________.
   a) ☐ Australia
   b) ☐ Great Britain
   c) ☐ New Zealand

5. Sandra Williams is Linda's ______________.
   a) ☐ cousin
   b) ☐ sister
   c) ☐ colleague

Inspector Robert Kenny decides to do the questioning.
"Hello, Mandy. May I call you Mandy?"
Mandy smiles at him shyly.
"If you want to, Inspector. Are you married?"
Inspector Kenny goes red and looks at Kelly North for help.

Sergeant Kelly North *takes over*.
"Mandy. I'll ask the questions, if you don't mind?"
Mandy Farraday *pats* her hair and smiles again at Inspector Kenny.
"Mandy? You told us yesterday that you and your sister Linda *got on* quite well?"
Mandy smiles again, still looking at Robert Kenny.
"Yes, I did. I mean sometimes we argued, but nothing that most sisters don't do."
"I see. Well, Sandra Williams and Miss Dunbar see it differently."
Mandy looks at Kelly North for the first time and *sneers*.
"Sandra Williams and Miss Dunbar! What do they know? They have no idea what life is about."
"Why do you say that?"
"Miss Dunbar is just a *slave*. She never married and never has fun. She's just a dried-up old *spinster*."
"And Sandra Williams?"
"Oh, she's not worth talking about. She's *uneducated* and I know that she's secretly in love with Ned Taylor. She's just too stupid to do anything about it. She and Linda were always making plans to get me into trouble."
"So, you and Linda fought a lot?"
"Well, yes, but it doesn't mean I killed her."
"Who do you think killed Linda?"
"Ned Taylor, of course. He's *terrified* he'll lose his freedom. He wants to have fun, not be married."
"We were informed that you and Linda started fighting a lot after Mrs Farraday died."
"That's right. It was all Linda's fault, you know."
"What was Linda's fault?"
"Mum's death!"
"Did Linda kill her?" Sergeant North sounds surprised.

ÜBUNG 12

!

Übung: 12: Welche Wörter stehen miteinander in Zusammenhang?

1. scream	☐	bang
2. stiff	☐	assist
3. inform	☐	pause
4. help	☐	shout
5. stupid	☐	tell
6. crash	☐	silly
7. stop	☐	hard

"Not directly. Mum picked us up from school one day. Linda started a fight with me and started *pinching* me."

"What happened then?"

"I screamed and Mum turned round to tell us off. She didn't see another car coming out of a side street and we crashed right into it."

"Mandy, surely it was your *scream* that *caused* the accident?"

Mandy's *body* goes stiff and she starts to shout.

"I'm telling you it was Linda's fault! It was always Linda's fault! I'm daddy's good little girl."

Robert Kenny looks at Kelly North and gestures for her to take it easy.

"Okay, Mandy. We can see you're *upset*. Let's take a short break. Would you like something to drink?"

"A coke, please. I'm hungry, too."

Kelly North rings for a woman police *constable* to bring a coke and a sandwich. When she arrives, North and Kenny walk to the coffee machine in the hall.

"She's *a handful*, isn't she, Kelly?"

"She certainly is. How can she flirt and eat, when her sister died yesterday?" the sergeant shakes her head.

"Good question. Do you think she's a little crazy?"
"Either crazy – or *obsessed*. She's seventeen, but she acts as if she's ten."
"Yes, you're right."
They walk back to the interview room and Kelly North continues the questioning.
"Mandy. Did you go to school yesterday?"
"I wanted to, but my father said I shouldn't."
"Didn't you care that your sister was dead?"
"Not really."
Robert Kenny stands up and puts his hands on the table. "Miss Farraday. I don't believe I'm hearing this."
Mandy sits back in her chair, *stunned*.
"Now. What time did you get up yesterday?"
Mandy starts playing with the buttons on her coat. "About half past six."
"Are you sure?"
"Yes."
"How come Miss Dunbar saw you leaving the house at half past four?"
"What!"
Mandy looks away. Inspector Kenny's voice gets a little louder. "I'm waiting, Miss Farraday?"
"Oh, now I remember. I went to the bakery. I wanted to give daddy a nice surprise."
"Which bakery?"
"Bennets. It's only ten minutes walk from our house."
"Well, I don't know any bakery in London that opens before 6 a.m."
"That's right. They were closed, so I went home again."
"That's strange. We arrived at your house just after seven yesterday. Miss Dunbar said you got home ten minutes before us. So, it takes

you two and a half hours to walk to the bakery and home again. Didn't you say it was only ten minutes?"

Mandy Farraday starts to panic and gets hysterical.

"Okay, okay. I went to the Starlight to confront Linda. The night before, we argued about daddy. He promised her ten thousand pounds to continue her studies in New Zealand. That's all my money!"

"I would say it's your father's money. Did you see Linda?"

"Yes. She was just coming out of the door. She said that Ned knew about the baby and that she would marry him."

"So you followed her to the park?"

"Yes. I was in a *rage*. I knew she was meeting Ned there and I wanted to speak to him. To tell him not to marry her."

"Ned didn't come, right?"

"Right. I was hiding in some bushes behind the bench. I remember thinking: she gets everything. A handsome man, a baby, marriage and my ten thousand pounds."

"So what did you do?"

"While I was waiting, a jogger ran past. I saw Linda give him her flirty smile and I just *lost it*. I saw red. I saw a heavy branch on the ground, picked it up and *bashed* her on the back of the head."

Inspector Robert Kenny stands up.

"Miss Mandy Farraday. I'm *arresting* you on the *charge* of murder."

ÜBUNG 13 !

Übung 13: Übersetzen Sie die Aussagen ins Englische!

1. Ned Taylor besitzt eine Disco.

....

2. Linda wollte ihr Studium fortsetzen.

3. Mandy ist ein sehr eifersüchtiges Mädchen.

4. Dr. Farraday ist ein sehr konservativer Mann.

5. Es gibt drei oder vier Verdächtige.

6. Inspector Kenny hat Hochzeitstag.

CATCHING A BIG FISH

Sarah Trenker

Chapter 1: A Wet Morning

Detective Henry Ramsey was angry, very angry. He didn't even wait for his young partner, Susan Mitchell, to close the car door before he started off down the road towards the harbour. It was raining. Susan *groaned*. The windows of Henry's old Mercedes always *misted up* when it was wet, and it was a long drive from Poole to Shelterwind *Cove*.

"Not a very nice day," Susan said as she quickly pulled on her *safety belt*. She tried to find space for her feet among the old newspapers and empty plastic cups on the floor. "But nice to get out of town *for a change*."

"Nice?" Henry shouted. "What do you mean by nice? This is the south of England, not the Côte d'Azur! What could possibly be nice about walking across a cold beach to look at a water-filled boat? And it's going to be a *waste of time*. We will probably find out that some idiot of a tourist *sank* the boat last spring."

Susan didn't answer. In his mid fifties, Henry was still a handsome man in a rough sort of way. But when he was in a bad *mood*, he looked a bit like a boxer before a fight. Susan decided it was better to leave him alone. She cleaned the passenger window with her sleeve and looked out at the boats as they drove along the beach road.

Anyway, she knew the real reason for Henry's anger. All the other detectives were on the big Churchill *case*. When they left the police station at 9 a.m., the others were listening to a tape of the kidnapper's *demands*. Detective Morgan, Henry's least favourite person at

the office, did not help things. When he saw them walk by, he wished them a nice morning on the beach.
Neither of the detectives spoke again until they reached a little village, which marked about the halfway point between Poole and Shelterwind *Cove*. The narrow stone streets were almost empty. There were just a few old ladies under umbrellas, who were looking at postcards.

Übung 1: Welches Wort ist das „schwarze Schaf"? Unterstreichen Sie das nicht in die Reihe passende Wort!

ÜBUNG 1 !

1. rain, wet, water, sand
2. town, school, village, city
3. irritation, rage, happiness, anger
4. detective, shop assistant, policeman, inspector
5. whisper, shout, sing, worry
6. laugh, smile, cry, grin
7. car, lorry, bicycle, motorbike

"At least we won't *get caught up in* the usual crowd of tourists, now that the school holidays are over," Susan said. "It'll be easy to park..."
"Hmmph," came the impatient reply, as Henry *swerved* to miss a car which was coming out of one of the side roads. "Why didn't Chief Inspector Crawley ask us to help them find that millionaire James Churchill? That is far more important. Morgan is no good for jobs like that. He couldn't find a bowl of rice in a Chinese restaurant! It is a mystery to me how HE hopes to find the kidnapper without having to pay the *ransom*."
Again Henry *swerved*, this time to narrowly miss a duck that was sitting in the middle of the road.

"*Anyway*, why is he still at the station? He should be out looking for *clues*. Is he waiting for the kidnapper to send him another finger?"

Susan thought back to the *envelope* with Churchill's little finger and the tape which someone had put on the steps of the station the day before. "I hope not," she *mumbled*.

Henry took no notice of her. "I don't think anyone has even been down to the Royal Bath Hotel to look at Churchill's room – and he disappeared the day before yesterday! You don't need six people to listen to a tape recording! They are wasting time that could cost Churchill his life."

Detective Ramsey *sniffed* loudly. "One of the most exciting *cases* for a long time. We should be working on it, too. But no, they don't *trust* me since the accident. I get sent to look at *stranded* boats and see if I can find any dead *bodies*."

His partner *nodded*, but said nothing. What could she say? Since that horrible accident when the teen murderer had tried to get away...

It was *understandable* that Henry had been *upset*. Everyone at the office knew he liked his whisky, but for a while people thought he was an alcoholic. Even now, a year and a half later, their boss, Chief Inspector Crawley, still did not seem to want to give his old favourite much responsibility.

ÜBUNG 2 !

Übung 2: Unterwegs mit dem Auto: Welche Wörter gehören zusammen? Setzen Sie die richtige Ziffer ein!

1. safety	☐ windscreen
2. steering	☐ seat
3. petrol	☐ licence

4. zebra	☐ belt
5. traffic	☐ station
6. passenger	☐ mirror
7. misty	☐ light
8. rear-view	☐ crossing
9. driving	☐ wheel

In the empty car park at Shelterwind *Cove*, the two detectives pulled on their coats. Then they walked along the path past the small houses and down to the famous *horseshoe-shaped cove*.

Although there were about 15 small boats on the sand, it was easy to recognize the boat they were here to see. Next to the fishing boats, the shiny, red motorboat was as unusual as a mango in a box of apples.

"It doesn't look as though it was under water for very long," said Susan as they walked over to look at it.

"No, it doesn't," Henry agreed as he looked at a small hole in the *hull*. "But why didn't the owners *report* it? Or at least tell somebody about it?"

Something was not quite right here. Henry smiled for the first time that day. At last, something to *get his teeth into*. He felt better already. Why, it had even stopped raining!

Susan tied her long red hair back to stop it blowing into her face and waited for instructions.

"See if you can find anything on the beach near the boat," Henry said. "I'll have a look in the *cabin*."

Susan walked off and Henry climbed onto the boat. Inside the *cabin* there was very little water, which seemed to show the boat got to the beach soon after it hit the rock. *Obviously*, thieves had soon found the boat, as a lot of the boat's *equipment* was missing. There was an expensive-looking *rope* in the corner and Henry wondered why the visitors hadn't taken that. He examined it and realized that it was in a number of pieces. Something had been tied at the back of the *cabin* and then quickly cut free. Perhaps the people on the boat were *drug-runners*, he thought. The boat was not really big enough to cross the *Channel*, but perhaps it had picked up a package from a sailboat near the coast and then got into difficulty during the bad weather.

The only other things left on the boat were a few sweet *wrappers* which were swimming in a pool of seawater at the bottom of the *cabin*. Henry recognized the *wrappers* immediately. Only one shop in the whole of *Dorset* sold that *kind of* caramels. The sweet shop was one of the top places to visit on Poole *Quay*.

When Henry jumped off the boat, he found Susan with two fishermen – an older man with a boy of about sixteen.

"These two found the boat," she informed him.

"Is that so?" answered Henry. "When was that, then?"

The older of the two fishermen, who was wearing a bright yellow raincoat, answered. "Yesterday morning, when we came down to go fishing."

"And why didn't you phone the police until today?" Henry replied impatiently.

"We thought the owner would come back during the day," the fisherman said.

"And when he didn't, that's when Mrs Summer decided to tell the police," the second fisherman added. The way he said "Mrs Summer" made it clear that he was not at all pleased that she had phoned the police.

You still had enough time to take anything you liked from the boat, Henry thought but didn't say. Instead, he turned to Susan: "The boat has no name, so it will be quite difficult to find the owners, unless the owners *report* the loss themselves."

He turned back to the fishermen and added, "Do you know if there have been any *sudden* arrivals in the village? Especially people without cars?"

The older fisherman shook his head, but as he was about to say no, his teen *companion* interrupted.

"What about that couple and their father who are staying at Mrs Cole's bed and breakfast? They arrived yesterday *out of the blue*."

"They would hardly have come here in a boat," answered the first fisherman angrily. "You know the old man is very ill. Use some *common sense*."

The boy *blushed* and looked down.

"Well, thank you for your help *anyway*," Henry replied. "Susan, perhaps you could get the names and addresses of these two gentlemen? It is just a formality," he added when he saw the reaction of the fishermen. "We will probably not need to contact you again."

Übung 3: Beantworten Sie die folgenden Fragen zum Text!

ÜBUNG 3 !

1. Why do Susan and Henry drive to Shelterwind Cove?

____

2. Who do they see in the village they drive through?

____

3. Why did Henry start drinking too much?

____

4. What does Henry find on the boat?

____

5. Who is the owner of the bed and breakfast?

Chapter 2: Fishermen's Tales

As the two detectives walked up the hill, they noticed a lot of curtains move in the house windows.

News travelled fast in a small village like this, Henry thought. He was thus not surprised to see a *plump* woman of about his age in the door of the bed and breakfast hotel. She was waiting for them.

"You must be Mrs Cole," said Henry.

"Yes, and you must be the two detectives who have come to look at that boat on the beach."

"Detectives Ramsey and Mitchell," Henry smiled as he walked down the path lined with seashells. In the garden next to the house was a small sailboat. In the wind its *halyard* whipped noisily against the mast.

"Could you show me your *identity card*, please?"

Susan pulled out her ID and showed it to Mrs Cole, who studied it carefully before giving it back.

"You'd better come in," Mrs Cole said. She turned and walked into a small *lounge*. Henry and Susan followed her.

Susan giggled when she saw the big yellow flowers on the *wallpaper* and again when she saw the glass cats on the table.

"My goodness, this is the definition of an English bed and breakfast house," she *whispered* as Mrs Cole walked across to the windows to pull back the curtains.

"How many guests have you got at the moment, Mrs Cole?"

"Just Mr and Mrs Hardy and Mrs Hardy's father Mr Perry. They arrived from Salisbury early yesterday morning."

"Did they come by car?" asked Henry.
"I think they took a train to Bridport and then got into a taxi to come here. Mr Hardy had to almost carry Mr Perry upstairs. The poor man is very ill. I think they've taken him to the doctor this morning. I haven't heard anyone upstairs."
"And have you had any other *sudden* visitors over the last couple of days?"
"No."
"Are you the only bed and breakfast in the village?" Henry asked. Susan giggled again.
"Mrs Penny also has a couple of rooms. She is four doors further down."
"Thank you for your help, Mrs Cole." Henry gave the woman his card.
"If you remember anything else that you think might be helpful, please let me know. We might come back and ask Mr and Mrs Hardy some questions later."

*Übung 4: Kennen Sie den Unterschied zwischen **much, many** und **a lot of**? Unterstreichen Sie das im Kontext richtige Wort!*

ÜBUNG 4 !

1. There were not much/many boats on the beach.
2. Mrs Hardy asked Mrs Cole how much/many visitors she had.
3. Harry didn't think it would be much/many fun on the beach in the rain.
4. How much/many people can you get in the boat?
5. How much/many diesel does the tank hold?
6. Harry drank many/a lot of whisky after the accident.
7. James Churchill has many/a lot of money.
8. Much/A lot of people live in Poole.

For the next hour, the two detectives walked from one house to the next and tried to find out if anyone had seen or heard anything. First, they visited the other bed and breakfast, but the two couples staying with Mrs Penny were both very old and therefore unlikely motorboat thieves. Afterwards, the two detectives separated and worked along opposite sides of the street. Nobody seemed to know anything, but everyone had a theory.

Susan laughed when she met Henry at the end of Sea View Road. "One more story about how easy it is to *sink* a boat here in winter and I shall start to give everyone medals."

Henry *snorted*. "I still can't help thinking that *there is more to this case than meets the eye*."

He glanced up to see the younger of the two fishermen watching them from one of four small houses on the hill. When the boy saw the two detectives look in his *direction*, he turned away and quickly walked inside.

Susan looked at Henry and *grinned*. Henry *grinned* back. "Now doesn't he look like someone with something useful to say?"

"Oh yes," agreed Susan.

ÜBUNG 5 !

Übung 5: Simple Present oder Present Continuous? Setzen Sie die Verben in Klammern in die richtige Zeitform!

1. Henry and Susan ______________ (drive) to work every day.
2. The fishermen ______________ (fish) in the cove at the moment.
3. Mrs Davies usually ______________ (rent) rooms to tourists.
4. The people in Shelterwind village ______________ (eat) a lot of fish.

5. Look out of the window and tell me if she ______________ (still smile)?

6. Mrs Cole ______________ (come) on Thursdays.

7. Two older couples ______________ (stay) at Mrs Penny's bed and breakfast.

8. Nobody ______________ (seem) to know anything.

When the two detectives knocked on the door, they heard a lot of worried whispering before the young fisherman opened the door. He looked nervous.

"Hello, detectives," he said. "Have you had any luck? Were the tourists any help?"

"No, *I'm afraid not*," answered Henry. He checked the name Susan had written down in her notebook on the beach. "We hoped you might be able to give us a bit more information, Mr Bridges."

"Me?"

A woman came up behind the boy with a *tea towel* in her hand. She understood the situation at once. "So what's our Tom been doing this time?" She was *obviously* the young man's mother.

"I don't know that Tom has been doing anything wrong, Mrs Bridges. We just wanted to ask him a few questions. He and Mr...", Henry looked again at the notebook, "Lambert were very helpful a bit earlier on this morning. We are trying to find out who owns the boat *stranded* on the beach and what it is doing here."

"Should Tom go and get Dave Lambert? He lives next door."

"That will not be necessary, Mrs Bridges." Henry put on one of his most winning smiles. "We can always go and see Mr Lambert if necessary." Susan nodded.

Übung 6: Lesen Sie weiter und setzen Sie die richtigen Präpositionen ein!
(at, in, into, to (5x), from, for, of)

Mrs Bridges *nodded* and asked them (1.) _____ follow her. They went (2.) _____ the kitchen and sat round the kitchen table (3.) _____ the corner.

"I don't know what you want me (4.) _____ tell you now," Tom *muttered*. "I told you everything I know this morning."

Henry *got straight to the point*. "Mr Bridges, I have reason to believe that someone may have taken some (5.) _____ the things that were on the boat."

Tom suddenly found his tea and the sugar bowl very interesting.

"That, of course, makes it very difficult (6.) _____ me to know where the boat came from and who it belonged (7.) _____," Henry continued. "It makes me think that it might not be just *theft* we are looking (8.) _____, but murder. An intelligent murderer would remove all the *evidence* (9.) _____ the boat, so that it would be difficult (10.) _____ *trace* the boat back (11.) _____ the owner."

"Are you saying you think my son is a murderer?" Mrs Bridges *exclaimed* angrily.

"Mrs Bridges, I think the fact that the boat has been *picked clean* does make the whole thing look *suspiciously* like murder."

Tom stopped *stirring* his tea. “I didn’t have anything to do with any murder, honest!” Tom *hesitated*. “I might have taken a couple of things off the boat... The *insurance* will pay the owner – so, we... er... I decided to save some of the things that were still on it.”
Mrs Bridges looked at Tom angrily. “What were you thinking, Tom? Go and get all of those things now.”
“I can’t. I don’t have the stuff any longer.”
“Where is it?” Mrs Bridges stood up. Henry interrupted her before she could continue.
“Mrs Bridges, perhaps I should speak to your son alone for a while. It is very important that I find out exactly what he has done. *Obviously*, *theft* is not as serious as *piracy*!”
It was Mrs Bridges’s turn to look nervous. “*Piracy*?” she *muttered*.
Susan saved the situation. “Mrs Bridges, perhaps you and I could talk together next door. I have some questions for you.”

Übung 7: Setzen Sie die passenden Krimi-Wörter ein!
(knife, body, evidence, kidnapper, rope, ransom)

1. Henry found a piece of ______________ on the boat.
2. They hid the ______________ money at the bottom of the garden behind the big tree.
3. The police caught the ______________ the next day
4. They found Mrs Penny’s ______________ at the bottom of the pond.
5. The lawyer had enough ______________ to win the case.
6. The wounds on the body showed that the murderer had used a ______________.

When the two were alone in the room, Henry took out his notebook and put it on the table.

“Tom, I don’t think you had anything to do with the missing crew, but taking things from a boat that doesn’t belong to you is still a serious crime. What has happened to the things you took?” Henry asked.

“We took them to Weymouth. We met someone there that can sell the stuff.”

“We?” Henry lifted an eyebrow.

Tom *shuffled his feet* nervously. “Dave Lambert and I occasionally sell the things we... find.”

“And Dave Lambert is the man we saw with you this morning,” said Henry.

“Yes, that’s right.”

Henry closed his notebook, the new page still clean, and put it in his pocket. “I think it is perhaps time to go and speak to your friend Mr Lambert.”

The boy *groaned*. “He’ll kill me...”

“He’s not allowed to do that,” replied Henry. “But don’t worry; if he does kill you, I’ll *arrest* him.” Henry smiled to himself as he saw Tom’s face.

ÜBUNG 8

Übung 8: Trifft die Aussage zu? Markieren Sie mit richtig ✔ oder falsch – !

1. Mrs Cole was a slim woman. ☐
2. Susan liked the decoration in the lounge of the bed and breakfast. ☐
3. There are two bed and breakfast hotels in Shelterwind Cove. ☐

4. Henry and Susan stayed together when they questioned the other people in the village. ☐
5. Mrs Bridges was Tom Bridges's wife. ☐
6. Tom is a teenager. ☐
7. Henry doesn't think Tom has anything to do with the missing crew. ☐
8. Tom is a bit afraid of Dave Lambert. ☐
9. Tom did not take anything from the boat. ☐

Although Henry was sure that Tom had had nothing to do with the disappearance of the crew from the boat, he was not as sure about Dave Lambert.

When Henry and Susan came to question him, the man was very aggressive and spoke in a deep, unpleasant voice that made him sound very dangerous. One look from him had been enough to make Tom be quiet.

"Like Tom said, we only took things from the boat after we found it on the beach," he *growled*. "I took the stuff into Weymouth and found a man staying in the *marina* who bought it from me. That's why I can't tell you where to find him. I didn't ask his name and he wanted to leave the next day."

Henry was sure that there was something that the fishermen were not telling them, but it seemed useless to question Dave Lambert any further.

As the two detectives left the house, Henry noticed a taxi parked in the porch. He looked at the fisherman.

"Did you find that, too?"

Lambert *scowled*. "No, that's mine. When fishing is bad, I earn a bit of extra money with the taxi. I have a licence. Do you want to see it?"

Detective Ramsey shook his head. He looked at the fisherman.

"We need to find the owners of the boat. I think they may be *drug-runners*. Lives may be in danger. Please tell me if you remember anything else about the man who bought the things from the boat."

The two detectives started to walk slowly back towards the car park. They were silent for a couple of minutes, then Susan *muttered*, "I'm not sure Dave Lambert told us all he knew."

"That makes two of us," answered Henry.

"*Piracy used to be* very *common* in these parts, didn't it?" asked Susan after a few minutes.

"Yes. In the old days, the people here *used to guide* the ships onto the rocks, kill the crew and then take all the *cargo*."

"Well, then I *suppose* we should be happy their great grandchildren are continuing their trade on a less murderous level," answered Susan.

"If only we could be sure," *muttered* Henry. Susan nodded but said nothing.

As they were about to drive out of the car park, Tom ran towards them. Henry opened his window.

"You forgot your notebook, Detective Ramsey," the boy said loudly.

Henry was about to say his notebook was in his pocket when he saw the boy's worried face.

"Thank you, Tom," he replied equally loudly and took a piece of paper from Tom's hand.

"I didn't give you this," Tom *whispered*.

"And nobody here will ever know, but I shall remember," Henry replied quietly and drove off, leaving the boy standing alone in the car park.

"What is it?" Susan asked as Henry opened the piece of paper with one hand.

"If I'm right, it is the name of the man we need in Weymouth."

Henry was right. It was.

Chapter 3: Back in Town

On the way to Weymouth, Susan contacted Poole police station to let them know where they were and to find out if anyone had *reported* the boat missing in the meantime. Nobody had.

There was also nothing good to *report* on the Churchill *case*. The only new piece of information was that it appeared that James Churchill was not in the hotel at all at the time of the kidnapping. A man at the Royal Bath Hotel had seen him leave the hotel on foot at about 5 p.m. Otherwise, the only other news was that Churchill's manager in Poole, Russell Davies, was causing problems. He now phoned Richard Morton almost every hour to ask him to hurry up and hand over the *ransom* money. He knew from Churchill's son that the *ransom* money was already at the police station. He shouted angrily at Richard Morton every time he phoned.

"Probably because he is very worried about Churchill," said Susan when she told Henry about the phone call. "Churchill's son delivered the money almost immediately, so he can't understand why Morton hasn't organized a meeting with the kidnapper."

"Poor old Morton," Henry remarked, smiling. "I *bet* he wishes he could come to Weymouth with us now."

It was not hard to find the place on Tom's note. The "fish and bits" shop was the main *centre of attention* on the *quay*. It was clearly popular with both fishermen and hobby sailors and was *bursting with* every *kind of* man and woman of the water. With so many people inside, it was difficult for the detectives to see who was *in charge*.

Eventually, however, a *bearded* man in a *Breton sweater* came over to help them.

"Can I help you?"

Henry *nodded* and held up his police *badge*.

The man's smile disappeared. "What's wrong?" he asked nervously.

"Are you the owner of this shop?" Henry quickly put away his ID and got out his notebook.

"Yes. My name is Bert Collins."

"Mr Collins, we have reason to believe that you recently bought some second-hand boat parts which were on a boat *stranded* at Shelterwind *Cove*. Is that right?"

"Yes, that is right, from two local fishermen, who said they got the parts from an old boat that did not belong to anybody."

"That is not quite true," smiled Henry, who realized that the owner probably often bought boat parts from people who "found" them somewhere.

Customers were looking in their *direction* now. "I have the box out the back," said Bert and led the two detectives to a small room behind the shop. On the table was a cardboard box. "This is the stuff they brought me," he *grunted*.

"Is this all?" asked Henry. The box seemed very small. He looked into the box and waited for the man to *comment*, but he didn't.

"I will have to take this box with me," he added.

"I paid good money for this *equipment*", said the manager angrily, "and have the receipt to prove it."

"Mr Collins, do you know the difficulties you could get into if I *reported* the fact that you bought stolen goods to sell in your shop?"

"How was I *supposed* to know that the fishermen stole these goods?"

Susan *snorted* and Henry laughed as he picked up the box. "I hope for you, Mr Collins, that everything is in this box, or there will be trouble... I would also advise you not to tell either of the two fishermen that we have picked up their box. Otherwise I will have to *assume* that you often buy stolen goods..."

Bert Collins *swallowed* hard and shook his head. “I won’t say a word,” he promised.

Übung 9: Wie lautet das Gegenteil? Setzen Sie die richtige Vorsilbe ein, um die Sätze zu vervollständigen!
(dis-, im-, un- (3x), mis-)

1. Henry Ramsey did not like Detective Morgan. He ___ liked him.
2. It was not pleasant to listen to the man’s voice. The voice was ___ pleasant.
3. Mrs Cole is not a patient woman. She is ___ patient.
4. Not all the information the detectives find is important. Sometimes information is ___ important.
5. Tom did not immediately understand what Detective Ramsey wanted. Tom ___ understood him.
6. Dave Lambert is not very happy. He is ___ happy.

On the way back to Poole police station, Henry asked Susan to phone Mrs Bridges. “Tell her to *remind* her son and Dave Lambert that they are now responsible for making sure nothing else happens to that boat. If the owner appears, they should get his or her name and phone me immediately. Nobody may move the boat. Perhaps a team from the *drug squad* should go across to the village,” he finished. “I’ll talk to Inspector Crawley about it this afternoon.”
The two detectives got back to Poole police station at lunchtime. Their colleagues seemed to be in almost exactly the same position

they had been in at 9 a.m. However, the noisy activity was now a worried silence as the detectives waited for the telephone to ring.
"Hi, Richard. Have you had a nice morning in the office?" Henry asked.
Richard *frowned* and ignored the question.
Just at that moment, the telephone rang. Everyone jumped. Richard Morton signalled to a colleague and they both picked up a phone *receiver* at the same time.
"Hello, Detective Morton speaking."
A digitally *disguised* voice thundered through the loudspeaker of the telephone. "Detective Morton, how nice! Have you got the little package ready for me yet? I know you want to *transfer* the money as soon as possible." The sarcasm was *obvious*.
"We are worried about Mr Churchill," said Detective Morton, without answering the question. "We do not want to do the exchange on Brownsea island. It will take us too long to get Mr Churchill to hospital."
"Of course, how *thoughtful* of you."
Everyone watched the computer as it tried to find the caller, but as soon as it seemed to have the location, the location moved again.
"If you try to *trace* this call, you will not succeed," the man continued. Then there was the sound of a hand *banging* on a table. "I am getting a bit angry with you, Detective Morton. You have had my instructions for over 24 hours. You have *wasted* time and I don't like that. To show you just how much I don't like *wasting* time, I have sent you another package. That may convince you that I am serious in my threat to kill Churchill if you do not come up with the money this evening. Rather sad really, if you consider how well Churchill plays the piano – or should I say PLAYED...?"
The line went silent for a couple of seconds except for a strange *whipping* noise in the background.

"Have you understood me, Morton?"
"Loud and clear," replied Detective Morton *grimly*.
The line went dead. Detective Morton looked over at his colleague at the computer, who shook his head.
"*Damn*! We're back to where we started. And it sounds like Churchill has lost another finger."
Henry was *thoughtful* for a moment. "Richard, that *whipping* noise. Do you know what it is?"
Richard looked up. "No, but it is there every time he rings, which would seem to confirm that he is not moving location."
"I know that sound from somewhere," said Henry. "I only wish I could remember where."
"That makes two of us," answered Richard. The two men smiled at each other for the first time in months.
A worried secretary came in. She had a package in her hands. "This one was outside on the wall, too," she said.

Übung 10: Übersetzen Sie die Begriffe, um das Rätsel zu lösen!

ÜBUNG 10 !

1. Hintergrund _ _ _ ☐ _ _ _ _ _ _
2. Opfer _ ☐ _ _ _ _
3. Mord _ _ _ ☐ _ _
4. Lösegeld _ _ ☐ _ _ _
5. Sarkasmus _ _ _ _ ☐ _ _
6. Piraterie ☐ _ _ _ _ _
7. Polizist ☐ _ _ _ _ _ _ _ _
8. Stehlen _ _ ☐ _ _
9. Detektiv ☐ _ _ _ _ _ _ _ _

Lösung: _ _ _ _ _ _ _ _ _

Henry left Richard and his team with the second parcel and was suddenly glad that he didn't have anything to do with the Churchill *case*. He and Susan went to his office and emptied the contents of the box onto his desk.

Susan picked up a *brass barometer*. "There is a small name plate on this. Perhaps that might help us to find the owner."

"Can you read it?"

Susan held it under a lamp. "Well it's pretty old. The *brass* has been cleaned so often that the name plate is almost impossible to read. It seems it was a prize for a sailing *competition*. Yes, that's it. 'Winner of the 18th Brownsea Island Regatta, 1978.' There is no name."

"Well, it is a start at least," answered Henry. "Phone the Poole sailing clubs and find out which of them does a Brownsea Island Regatta. They should have lists of the winners for the last few years."

While Susan was making the phone calls, Henry looked at the other items from the box. He picked up a GPS. He was no sailor, but he knew enough about GPS systems to wonder whether the person *in charge of* the boat had used *waypoints* to help him get from one place to the other. He turned the GPS on and played with it for a while until he found the *waypoint* programme.

"I've found it," he *exclaimed*.

Susan eyed him *suspiciously*. "What is it? Have you found a name?"

"No, not quite as good as that but almost. I have found the *waypoints* for the last trip. The boat left from the new *marina* on Poole *quay*. That *marina* is quite small, so we might find someone there who knows the boat."

Henry picked up the phone and rang *directory enquiries*. A woman gave him the telephone number of the *marina* and then connected him. A man answered the phone.

"Poole *Quay Marina*."
"Hello, this is Detective Ramsey from the Poole police station. I am phoning concerning a boat we found on the beach in Shelterwind *Cove*. I am hoping you might be able to help me find out who the owners are."
"What *kind of* boat is it?"
"It is a bright red motorboat, one of those new French boats everybody has been talking about, Jeanmoreau, Jeaneau or something like that... It left your *marina* at about 2 p.m. two days ago."
The man at the other end of the line thought for a moment, while Henry *crossed his fingers*.
"Yes, I know the one you mean," the man said suddenly. "That is the 'Carpe Diem'. It belongs to the Poole *branch* of Witan Holdings, but sometimes other people take it out. This time it was a man and his wife. They told me that they would be away for a couple of days, so I should not expect to see them before Sunday."
"Who told you they could take the boat out?"
"Russell Davies."
"Thank you very much!" Henry put down the phone.
Susan had also just put down the *receiver*. "Hurrah! I've got the name..." she shouted.
"Russell Davies *by any chance*?" asked Henry.
"*Damn* you," Susan laughed. "Hey, isn't Russell Davies the name of James Churchill's manager down here?"
"It is indeed!"

Übung 11: Formulieren Sie die Sätze im Simple Past!

ÜBUNG 11 !

1. The detective finds a clue on the beach.

____

2. It takes a long time to get from Poole Harbour to Shelterwind Cove.

3. Fishermen from Shelterwind Cove sell their fish at the market in Weymouth.

4. Dave Lambert goes fishing every day, but he also steals equipment from the boats he finds on the beach.

5. The kidnapper cuts off the victim's finger.

6. He puts the finger into an envelope and sends it to Poole police station.

Chapter 4: In the Net

Inspector Crawley's office at the police station always seemed like a palace compared with the small offices the rest of the team worked in. Henry had asked to speak to both him and Richard Morton about his *latest* discovery.

"So you mean to tell me that a boat that belongs to Witan Holdings

disappeared on the same day as Churchill, and Russell Davies forgot to mention it?"
"Well, it could be that he hasn't even realized that it has gone missing if the man and woman said that they would be away until Sunday," Susan *commented*.
"It could be," answered Inspector Crawley and looked at Richard Morton for his opinion.
"I agree with Susan," said Richard Morton. "Witan Holdings is an *enormous* company. It has come a long way since James Churchill opened the first *branch* in Dover. Now he has companies in all major *coastal* towns. The *headquarters* of Witan Holdings is in London – and Churchill's son will *take over* from his father next year."
"The *branch* in Poole is very small. Why did James Churchill come down here?" asked Inspector Crawley.
"He is *tying up loose ends*. He wants to make sure his son does not have too many problems when he *takes over* the business. He is closing some of the less profitable businesses. Poole might be on the list."
"Could he have been out on the motorboat?"
Richard Morton laughed. "No! He is almost seventy. The missing boat is probably just a *coincidence*."
"But I'm pretty sure that this is NOT just a *coincidence*! There is a connection between the two *cases* and I would like to be able to *follow it up*," said Henry.
Inspector Crawley thought for a moment and then looked straight at Henry. "OK, Henry. I think Richard and his team have enough problems here at the moment. You and Susan should find out what happened to the two people on the boat and whether the *coincidence* involving Mr Davies and that boat in Shelterwind Cove is actually a connection."

Übung 12: Übersetzen Sie die Wörter ins Deutsche!

1. discovery ______________
2. to mention ______________
3. connection ______________
4. coincidence ______________
5. case ______________
6. to happen ______________
7. clue ______________
8. telephone receiver ______________

Half an hour later, Henry and Susan drove into Witan Holdings in Poole. The car park at the building was full of birds – a sure sign that some really windy weather was on its way.

"What does Witan do?" Susan asked.

"Something in the *maritime* business," Henry answered. "Quite an old firm, but apparently it has been having money problems recently. There has even been talk that James Churchill was thinking of selling the company and that he was in Poole to talk to Russell Davies."

"Russell Davies must be worried!"

"Yes, I *suppose* so."

The woman at the reception *showed them in*. Russell Davies had an *enormous* office, which did not seem to have any money problems. On the floor there was an expensive-looking carpet, old paintings of ships at sea hung on the walls and Russell Davies was sitting behind a large *Chippendale* desk.

James Churchill's partner did not stand to greet the detectives but *waved* them to two seats opposite his desk while he finished a phone call.

When he put the phone down, Russell Davies *got straight down to business*. "Hello Detectives. I hope you are here to tell me that you will soon be able to give the kidnappers the money. I know the *headquarters* in London have already *transferred* the money. I think you have already *wasted* enough time. James has suffered enough."

Henry looked for a sign of sympathy to *match* the words but found none. Russell Davies was a hard businessman, he decided. He was a man who expected things to be done correctly and immediately.

"Detective Morton is waiting for the final instructions from the kidnapper. Then we will do the exchange. Have you had any phone calls from the kidnapper?"

"No."

"We are here to ask about another *matter*. Has one of Witan's boats been *reported* missing?"

"Missing? No. What do you mean?" For a moment Russell Davies looked *concerned*.

"We have found one of your boats on the beach at Shelterwind *Cove*. There was no sign of the crew and we are worried that someone might have been hurt."

Russell Davies *frowned*. "I see. I *lent* the boat to a couple of people from Norway. They phoned me yesterday to tell me that there had been a problem, but I was too busy to listen to what they had to say, *I'm afraid*."

"I need to talk to them," said Henry. "They can't just walk off and leave a boat half *floating* in the water. It is very dangerous."

"You are right of course, Detective. But, as you know, I have had a lot to think about over the last few days."

"Yes, I do *appreciate* that. Could you give me the names of the two people who took the boat? I must talk to them."
Russell Davies *hesitated*. "I don't have their number here. I will get my secretary to give it to you later on today."
"That would be good, Mr Davies. I shall wait for her call."
Henry stood up. "Thank you for your time. Come on, Susan."
Susan stood up and walked over to *admire* one of the paintings as Henry put on his coat. "What lovely pictures you have in here," she smiled, her hand on the frame of one of the paintings.

ÜBUNG 13 !

Übung 13: Lesen Sie weiter und bilden Sie sinnvolle Wörter aus dem Buchstabenchaos!

Outside, Henry turned to Susan, "So did you manage to *bug* the room while we were (1. tikgnla) ________________?"
Susan (2. slemid) ________________. "But of course, Henry. One on the phone and one on that big painting on the wall. What lovely pictures he has... What a joke! They're almost as boring as he is."
She giggled.
Henry *grinned*. "We'd better drive around the (3. creron) ________________ – *just in case* he is watching us from his window."
Susan *nodded* in agreement.
Out of *sight* of the building, the (4. dictvcstec) ________________ parked next to a shop and turned on the *receiver*. For about five (5. metisun) ________________, there was nothing *suspicious* about

Russell Davies' behaviour. He told his secretary to organize some

(6. getimens) _______________ and send some letters.

However, as soon as she left the room, Russell Davies picked up the phone.

There was a pause as the telephone rang at the other end and somebody answered.

"I thought you said the boat *sank*," Russell Davies said angrily.

"Well, we thought it did." The woman at the end of the phone was nervous.

"Give me Paul!"

The *receiver* was passed from one hand to another.

"Yep. What do you want?"

The man's voice was hard and unpleasant.

"You told me the boat *sank*."

"That was the original plan. But it got changed. It wasn't my idea."

"Two detectives asked me about the boat. They even went to Shelterwind *Cove* to look at it – and they want YOUR names. We are running out of time. We are going to have to leave the country sooner than we thought."

"Yeah, I know." The man laughed.

"Where are you?"

"We're safe for the moment. That's all you need to know. My brother helped us find somewhere safe before the idiot almost *blew* everything."

The man's voice got louder. "Now, you just make sure we get the money. I only got two fingers from the *morgue*, so next time I really will have to cut off one of Churchill's fingers. The *ransom* must be delivered this evening, or we will have to *call* everything *off*. So phone the police station again and get things moving."

The line went dead.

ÜBUNG 14 !

Übung 14: Adjektiv oder Adverb? Unterstreichen Sie die richtige Variante!

1. He was a suspicious/suspiciously man.
2. He eyed them suspicious/suspiciously.
3. He can't play football very good/well.
4. He will have to study hard/hardly to pass the exams.
5. Mistakes easy/easily happen.
6. The woman spoke very fast/fastly.

A group of teens walked out of the shop. They met a woman outside whom they *obviously* knew and started talking to her. The *sight* seemed strange after listening to the kidnapper, Susan thought.

"If only we knew where they were," she *muttered* angrily.

"Oh, but we do," answered Henry suddenly. "Of course!" he shouted and hit the *steering wheel*. "But there isn't a minute to *waste*. Call up the station. Get them to send a couple of officers round to 'look after' Russell Davies. They should tell him that it is for his own safety. Whatever happens, the officers must not let him out of their *sight*, or allow him to make any more telephone calls. We don't want him to make any other bad decisions, do we?"

Susan was *confused*. "And where are we going?"

"Shelterwind *Cove*! But first I need to speak to Inspector Crawley and Detective Morton. We'll stop at the police station on our way."

Thirty minutes later, the old Mercedes was back on the road towards Shelterwind *Cove*. Henry felt nervous and happy at the same time. Now it all made sense: the *whipping* sound in the background when the kidnapper spoke to Richard Morton, the similar voices, the taxi driver. It seemed impossible that he had missed it before, but of course he had been looking for a boat thief, not a kidnapper.

Henry parked in the main car park again. There were three other cars there which belonged to a large group of *hikers*. One of them looked up as Henry got out of the car smiling.

"Not the nicest of evenings for a hike," Henry said loudly.

"No, not really," answered one of the *hikers* equally loudly. "We only plan to walk to the hotel-pub at Shepherd's Lear tonight and then carry on tomorrow. Do you know the quickest way to get there, *by any chance*?"

"No, but Dave Lambert would know. He's a fisherman here and knows this area well. He lives in that house over there, the one with the taxi in the garage."

"Thank you." The *hiker winked* and *set off* to Dave Lambert's house with three of his *companions*.

Susan was feeling slightly sick as they walked down the beach path towards Mrs Cole's bed and breakfast. Henry looked at her.

"Would you prefer to go and speak to Tom Bridges again?" he asked in a low voice.

"No." Susan's *expression hardened*. "I won't *let you down*. You don't have to worry."

Detective Ramsey *nodded* and smiled *grimly*. "Good. Everybody ready then," he *muttered* as if to himself. He and Susan entered the gate of the bed and breakfast. It was still quite windy; the *halyard* of the small boat in the garden was *banging* against the house wall again and making its strange *whipping* sound.

Übung 15: Setzen Sie den richtigen Begriff in die Lücke ein!
(mast, cove, cargo, quay, halyard, hull)

1. The products that a boat carries: ____________

2. On a boat, this holds up the sail: ____________

3. A rope that pulls up a sail: ____________

4. Boats can tie up here: ____________

5. The bottom of a boat: ____________

6. A place on the coast with some shelter from the wind: ____________

Mrs Cole looked a bit impatient when she saw the two detectives at the door.

"Are you back again? I thought I'd answered all your questions this morning."

"You did, Mrs Cole, but as I said this morning, we would still like to speak to Mr and Mrs Hardy."

"Well, come in then." Mrs Cole took them back into the small *lounge*.

"Please tell Mr and Mrs Hardy that I need to speak to BOTH of them," said Henry.

Mrs Cole walked in a couple of minutes later with a man and a woman, both of whom looked about 35. They looked *tense* and had their hands in their pockets.

"Detective Ramsey, this is Mr and Mrs Hardy. I have told them that you just needed to ask them a couple of questions."

"Thank you Mrs Cole, it was very kind of you to bring them in," answered Henry, smiling *firmly*.

Mrs Cole understood the message. "Yes, right then, I'll be in the kitchen if you need me." With that she left the *lounge* and closed the door behind her.

Henry held out a hand to Mr Hardy. "Good evening."

"How can we help you?" asked Mr Hardy, ignoring Henry's hand, his right hand *firmly* in his right-hand pocket. "We were just about to go out, now that my father-in-law *is asleep* at long last."

"You arrived here yesterday, Mrs Cole tells me. Is that correct?" Henry asked.
"Yes, we got a taxi from Bridport station and arrived yesterday morning," answered the woman. She was looking nervously at the man who stood next to her. He *frowned* at her.
"We would have been here a lot earlier if her father hadn't needed to stop the taxi every five minutes because he wasn't feeling well," her husband *growled*. "But *anyway*, why do you need to know?"
The man tried to smile, but he only managed a grimace.
Something broke in the kitchen and the noise made the man turn *briefly* towards the door.
Henry used the opportunity. He threw himself at the man and pushed him back onto the floor. Mr Hardy put his hand to his pocket but stopped as he saw the two guns that were pointed at him.
"Oh shit," he *muttered* angrily and put his hands up.
At the same moment, the door opened and two of the *hikers burst in*, both with guns in their hands.
"Everything under control, Detective Ramsey?"
"I think he has a gun in his pocket," answered Henry.
One of the *hikers* quickly removed a weapon from the man's pocket and put *handcuffs* on him.
The woman started crying. "I always told you it was a bad idea," she said and put her hands up, too. Susan walked over to her and removed a small gun from her pocket.
Everything suddenly seemed to be moving very fast and the small house seemed even smaller. Mrs Cole was shouting angrily in the kitchen, while a large number of what looked like *hikers*, but were in fact *special force* policemen, rushed up the narrow *staircase* to the rooms upstairs.
"We found him," a man shouted down the stairs. "He is *drugged* but otherwise seems to be in good health."

"That's good for you, Mr Hardy, or should I call you Paul Lambert? That makes you Dave Lambert's brother, I believe?"

The handcuffed man *scowled*.

"Your brother provided you with the perfect alibi by driving you here in his taxi after you'd left the boat, didn't he? *Shame* he got *greedy* and decided not to *sink* the boat. I *suppose* you picked up James Churchill from the beach. Did he go there to buy some of those sweets Russell Davies told you he loved? That must have been easy. What did you give Churchill to make him sleep?"

"Sleeping pills. He'll be all right in a few hours," Lambert replied angrily. "*Anyway*, how did you find us so quickly? There was nothing left on the boat to provide you with any *clues*."

Henry looked at Susan. "Should I tell him?"

Susan shook her head. "Oh no, let him work it out. After all, he's going to have enough time to think about it, isn't he?"

Abschlusstest

Übung 1: Vervollständigen Sie die Aussagen zu „Waterloo Bridge"!

1. Marco hides from the police in a safe ________________.

2. Ali drives a white ________________.

3. Roberta's title is ________________.

4. Hadley's firm renovated Waterloo ________________.

5. Mr and Mrs Ibrahim have two small ________________.

6. Marco strangles the newsagent with ________________.

Übung 2: Vervollständigen Sie die Sätze mit den korrekten Verbformen!

1. Frank and Barry (be) ________________ two detectives.

2. Mrs Hutchinson (invite) ________________ the detectives to tea last Thursday.

3. The mayor (like, wear) ________________ elegant clothes.

4. Mr Monks (lose) ________________ his job because he (give) ________________ bank secrets to the investment experts.

5. Yesterday, Constable Jones (find) ________________ the body in the house.

6. The supermarket (open) ________________ every day at 9 a.m.

Übung 3: Was gehört zusammen? Setzen Sie die richtige Ziffer ein!

1. arrest	☐ a game
2. do	☐ for back-up
3. drive	☐ a post-mortem examination
4. call	☐ a motorbike
5. drink	☐ a criminal
6. ride	☐ a coffee
7. play	☐ a car

Übung 4: Beantworten Sie die folgenden Fragen zu „Murder in Battersea Park"!

1. Who saw Mandy leave the house very early?

____

2. Who has a surgery in Harley Street?

____

3. What was the man who found the body in the park doing?

____

4. What kind of studies did Linda want to continue?

____

5. How far is the bakery from the Farraday house?

____

6. Where does Sandra Williams work?

____

Übung 5: Welches Wort ist das „schwarze Schaf"?

1. newspaper, book, magazine, radio
2. elbow, neck, hand, arm
3. run, walk, jog, drive
4. murder, killing, kidnapping, weapon
5. daughter, son, aunt, sister
6. laugh, cry, smile, cough

Übung 6: Vervollständigen Sie die Sätze zu „Catching a Big Fish"!

1. Tom and Dave catch fish. They are ________________.
2. The money a kidnapper asks for is the ________________.
3. Boats usually have an instrument for measuring changes in the weather. It is a ________________.
4. A small hotel which only serves breakfast is a ________________.
5. Men who steal from boats at sea are ________________.

Übung 7: Welche Spuren aus dem Krimi „Catching a Big Fish" gehören zusammen? Setzen Sie die richtige Ziffer ein!

1. unpleasant	☐ barometer
2. red	☐ voice
3. brass	☐ halyard
4. young	☐ motorboat
5. telephone	☐ fisherman
6. banging	☐ call

Übung 8: Welcher Satz enthält die richtige Übersetzung?

1. Was meinst Du?
   a) ☐ What did you mean?
   b) ☐ What do you think?

2. Ich bin auf den Weg ins Polizeirevier.
   a) ☐ I am on the way to the police station.
   b) ☐ I am going in the police station.

3. Offensichtlich kannten sie die Frau.
   a) ☐ They obviously knew about the woman.
   b) ☐ They obviously knew the woman.

4. Die Frau fing an zu schreien.
   a) ☐ The woman started to shout.
   b) ☐ The woman started to cry.

Übung 9: Übersetzen Sie und enträtseln Sie das Lösungswort!

1. blass ☐ _ _ _
2. hupen _ ☐ _ _
3. tragisch _ _ _ _ ☐ _
4. streicheln ☐ _ _ _ _ _
5. einsam _ ☐ _ _ _ _
6. Krebs (Krankheit) ☐ _ _ _

Lösung: _ _ _ _ _ _

Lösungen

Terminus Waterloo Bridge

Übung 1: 1. a 2. b 3. a 4. b 5. b
Übung 2: 1. sea 2. cry 3. trousers 4. childs 5. feet 6. slim 7. motorbike
Übung 3: 1. I want to speak to Inspector Fletcher. 2. You aren't very polite. 3. Good morning, can I help you? 4. Why are you so nervous? 5. Ali gets out of the car. 6. He walks to the shop door and unlocks it.
Übung 4: 1. falsch 2. richtig 3. richtig 4. falsch 5. falsch 6. falsch
Übung 5: 1. outside 2. in 3. down 4. walk 5. old 6. death 7. men 8. white 9. good
Übung 6: 1. c 2. b 3. c 4. a 5. b
Übung 7: 1. I have an idea. 2. The computer produces five names. 3. Mrs Ibrahim answers the door. 4. Jack and Roberta enter the house. 5. Police cars are now arriving at the shop.
Übung 8: 1. red 2. yellow 3. blue 4. green 5. brown 6. white 7. black Lösung: Roberta
Übung 9: 1. down/up 2. top/bottom 3. wrong/right 4. dad/mum 5. leave/arrive 6. cry/laugh 7. cheap/expensive
Übung 10: 1. office 2. immediately 3. door 4. probably 5. shows 6. fingerprint 7. later
Übung 11: 1. Yes, Dr Bird works in the autopsy room. 2. Roberta calls the hospital to get the report of the post-mortem. 3. Clive Hadley owns a building company. 4. Roberta claps her hands because she finds out Marco's identity. 5. Jack gets Roberta a coffee. 6. Roberta calls up "method of killing".
Übung 12: 1. photo 2. man 3. sure 4. sister 5. win 6. upstairs 7. play
Übung 13: 1. living room 2. safe house 3. police officer 4. no problem 5. alarm bell 6. glove compartment 7. mobile phone 8. bedside table
Übung 14: 1. from 2. fastest 3. begun 4. running 5. bridge 6. jumps 7. running 8. grins
Übung 15: 1. police 2. family 3. engine 4. bodyguard 5. million 6. motorbike 7. disappear

A Nice Neighbourhood

Übung 1: 1. bigger, biggest 2. more comfortable, most comfortable 3. heavier, heaviest 4. colder, coldest 5. better, best 6. slower, slowest
Übung 2: 1. slim 2. butcher 3. dies 4. posters 5. case 6. interrupts
Übung 3: 1. Where did he use to work? 2. How did you use to get to work? 3. How did the detectives use to contact each other? 4. Where did people use to post their letters? 5. When did Mr Philips use to receive his patients in the village hall? 6. Which game did Barry use to play in his spare time?
Übung 4: 1. richtig 2. falsch 3. falsch 4. falsch 5. richtig 6. richtig

Übung 5: 1. chaotic 2. full 3. football 4. house 5. meal 6. thief
Übung 6: 1. ring 2. murderer 3. light 4. papers 5. get 6. documents 7. at 8. shows
Übung 7: 1. hate/dislike 2. murder/kill 3. mug/cup 4. happen/take place 5. say/remark 6. trio/three people
Übung 8: 1. House of Commons 2. husband 3. biscuits 4. job applications 5. lonely 6. friends 7. hesitates
Übung 9: 1. poison 2. mayor 3. lives 4. wearing 5. papers
Übung 10: 1. The mayor comes out to greet them. 2. His wrinkles show deep frustration. 3. Detective Durham does not like the mayor very much. 4. The detective finds warfarin in Miss Chambers's kitchen. 5. The bank manager fired Mr Monks when he learned of the insider trading.
Übung 11: 1. tell 2. steal 3. begin 4. think 5. know 6. can
Übung 12: 1. doesn't he 2. isn't he 3. doesn't he 4. didn't he 5. won't he 6. wouldn't it
Übung 13: 1. a 2. b 3. b 4. a 5. b

Murder in Battersea Park

Übung 1: 1. jogging 2. bench 3. handbag 4. pulse 5. snore 6. shower 7. anniversary
Übung 2: 1. home 2. protect 3. swim 4. young 5. bench 6. clothes 7. dog
Übung 3: 1. daughter 2. cup 3. night 4. argument 5. adopt 6. wife 7. pregnant
Übung 4: 1. empty 2. woman 3. open 4. show 5. ask 6. notebook 7. called 8. Tears
Übung 5: 1. Mr Taylor was at home at 6 a.m. this morning. 2. Inspector Kenny's assistant is called Sergeant Kelly North. 3. The name of the murdered girl is Linda Farraday. 4. Mr Taylor's disco is called Starlight. 5. The name of the woman who worked with Linda is Sandra Williams. 6. Mr Taylor wears a silver stud in his left ear.
Übung 6: 1. brought (bring) 2. hte (the) 3. wen (when) 4. baad (bad) 5. playt (played) 6. come (comes) 7. thems (them) 8. kup (cup) 9. Fery (very) 10. ani (any)
Übung 7: 1. d 2. g 3. f 4. b 5. e 6. a 7. c
Übung 8: 1. I am not the murderer. 2. I saw a woman walking a dog. 3. She was expecting my child. 4. What can his motive be? 5. It all seems too easy. 6. Sandra is in love with Ned.
Übung 9: 1. in 2. in 3. on 4. at 5. at 6. at, in 7. in 8. on
Übung 10: 1. safe 2. speak 3. really 4. girl 5. later 6. decide 7. leave 8. yesterday
Lösung: Farraday
Übung 11: 1. b 2. a 3. b 4. c 5. c
Übung 12: 1. scream/shout 2. stiff/hard 3. inform/tell 4. help/assist 5. stupid/silly 6. crash/bang 7. stop/pause
Übung 13: 1. Ned Taylor owns a disco. 2. Linda wanted to continue her studies. 3. Mandy is a very jealous girl. 4. Dr Farraday is a very conservative man. 5. There are three or four suspects. 6. It is Inspector Kenny's wedding anniversary.

Catching a Big Fish

Übung 1: 1. sand 2. school 3. happiness 4. shop assistant 5. worry 6. cry 7. bicycle

Übung 2: 1. safety belt 2. steering wheel 3. petrol station 4. zebra crossing 5. traffic light 6. passenger seat 7. misty windscreen 8. rear-view mirror 9. driving licence

Übung 3: 1. They drive to Shelterwind Cove to look at a boat found on the beach. 2. They see some women who are looking at postcards. 3. There had been a horrible accident with a teen murderer. 4. He finds a rope and some sweet wrappers. 5. The owner of the bed and breakfast is called Mrs Cole.

Übung 4: 1. many 2. many 3. much 4. many 5. much 6. a lot of 7. a lot of 8. A lot of

Übung 5: 1. drive 2. are fishing 3. rents 4. eat 5. is still smiling 6. comes 7. are staying 8. seems

Übung 6: 1. to 2. into 3. in 4. to 5. of 6. for 7. to 8. at 9. from 10. to 11. to

Übung 7: 1. rope 2. ransom 3. kidnapper 4. body 5. evidence 6. knife

Übung 8: 1. falsch 2. falsch 3. richtig 4. falsch 5. falsch 6. richtig 7. richtig 8. richtig 9. falsch

Übung 9: 1. dis- 2. un- 3. im- 4. un- 5. mis- 6. un-

Übung 10: 1. background 2. victim 3. murder 4. ransom 5. sarcasm 6. piracy 7. policeman 8. steal 9. detective Lösung: kidnapped

Übung 11: 1. The detective found a clue on the beach. 2. It took a long time to get from Poole Harbour to Shelterwind Cove. 3. Fishermen from Shelterwind Cove sold their fish at the market in Weymouth. 4. Dave Lambert went fishing every day, but he also stole equipment from the boats he found on the beach. 5. The kidnapper cut off the victim's finger. 6. He put the finger into an envelope and sent it to Poole police station.

Übung 12: 1. Entdeckung 2. erwähnen 3. Verbindung 4. Zufall 5. Fall 6. geschehen/passieren 7. Hinweis 8. Telefonhörer

Übung 13: 1. talking 2. smiled 3. corner 4. detectives 5. minutes 6. meetings

Übung 14: 1. suspicious 2. suspiciously 3. well 4. hard 5. easily 6. fast

Übung 15: 1. cargo 2. mast 3. halyard 4. quay 5. hull 6. cove

Lösungen Abschlusstest

Übung 1: 1. house 2. Golf 3. Inspector 4. Bridge 5. children 6. piano wire

Übung 2: 1. are 2. invited 3. likes to wear/wearing 4. lost, gave 5. found 6. opens

Übung 3: 1. arrest a criminal 2. do a post-mortem examination 3. drive a car 4. call for back-up 5. drink a coffee 6. ride a motorbike 7. play a game

Übung 4: 1. Miss Dunbar saw Mandy leave the house very early. 2. Dr Farraday has a surgery in Harley Street. 3. The man who found the body in the park was jogging. 4. Linda wanted to continue her medical studies. 5. The bakery is a ten minutes' walk from the Farraday house. 6. Sandra Williams works at the Starlight Disco.

Übung 5: 1. radio 2. neck 3. drive 4. weapon 5. son 6. cough

Übung 6: 1. fishermen 2. ransom 3. barometer 4. bed and breakfast 5. pirates

Übung 7: 1. unpleasant voice 2. red motorboat 3. brass barometer 4. young fisherman 5. telephone call 6. banging halyard

Übung 8: 1. b 2. a 3. b 4. a

Übung 9: 1. pale 2. honk 3. tragic 4. stroke 5. lonely 6. cancer Lösung: poison

GLOSSAR

fam	umgangssprachlich
fig	bildlich
pl	Plural
v	Verb

abuse	Beschimpfung; Missbrauch
according to	laut
admire *v*	bewundern
adopt *v*	adoptieren
amazement	Erstaunen
ammunition	Munition
amusement	Vergnügung, Unterhaltung
annoyed	verärgert
annual	jährlich
anyway	sowieso; dennoch; auf jeden Fall
application	Bewerbung
appreciate *v* **something**	dankbar sein
approach *v*	(sich) nähern
argument	Auseinandersetzung, Streit; Argument
armed	bewaffnet
arms dealer	Waffenhändler
arrest *v*	verhaften
assassin	Auftragsmörder, Attentäter
assassination	Ermordung, Attentat
assistance	Hilfe, Unterstützung
assume *v*	vermuten, annehmen
at full speed	mit voller Geschwindigkeit
at such short notice	so kurzfristig
available	verfügbar
back off *v*	zurückgehen, zurückweichen
back-up	Verstärkung
bad feeling	Verstimmung
badge	Abzeichen
bad-tempered	schlecht gelaunt
bang *v*	knallen, poltern
bankrupt *v*	(finanziell) ruinieren
barometer	Barometer, Luftdruckmesser

bash *v*	heftig schlagen
be (was, been) *v* **a handful** *fig*	schwierig sein
be (was, been) *v* **(fast) asleep**	(tief und fest) schlafen
be (was, been) *v* **miles away** *fig*	mit den Gedanken ganz woanders sein
be (was, been) *v* **terrified**	panische Angst haben
bearded	bärtig, mit Bart
bell	Klingel, Glocke
besides	außerdem
bet, bet, bet *v*	wetten
blame *v* **(s.o. for sth)**	beschuldigen, jemandem die Schuld an etwas geben
bless him *fam*	hier: die gute Seele
blow (blew, blown) *v* **something** *fam*	etwas vermasseln *fam*
blush *v*	rot werden, erröten
body	Körper; Leiche
bookshelves *pl*	Bücherregale
bother *v* **someone**	jemanden belästigen; stören
brake *v*	bremsen
branch	hier: Niederlassung; Ast
brass	Messing
Breton sweater	Matrosenpullover
briefly	kurz
brightly	hier: freudig, fröhlich; hell
bug *v*	verwanzen
burst (burst, burst) *v* **in**	hereinstürzen
burst (burst, burst) *v* **into tears**	in Tränen ausbrechen
burst (burst, burst) *v* **with**	überquellen von, platzen vor
by (any) chance	zufällig, durch Zufall
cabin	Kabine
call *v* **something off**	etwas abblasen, absagen
cancer	Krebs (Krankheit)
capable of	fähig (etwas zu machen)
cargo	Fracht
carnation	Nelke
case	Fall; Koffer
catch (caught, caught) *v* **fire**	Feuer fangen
catch (caught, caught) *v* **one's breath**	den Atem anhalten

cause *v*	verursachen
centre of attention	Zentrum der Aufmerksamkeit
chance	Chance, Gelegenheit; Zufall
change *v* **the subject**	das Thema wechseln
Channel	Ärmelkanal
charge	hier: Anklage; Auftrag; Last
cheat *v* **(on sb)**	(jemanden) betrügen
Chippendale furniture	teure Möbelmarke aus dem 18. Jahrhundert
choking noises *pl*	Würgegeräusche
chuckle *v*	glucksen, kichern
church-goer	Kirchgänger(in)
church hall	Gemeindehalle
clap *v*	klatschen
clear *v* **something up**	etwas (auf)klären
close-knit *fig*	eng verbunden *fig*
clue	Hinweis, Indiz
coastal	Küsten...
coincidence	Zufall
come (came, come) *v* **down a bit** *fam*	runterkommen *fam*
comment *v*	(etwas) kommentieren
commission	hier: Provision; Kommission
common	häufig, (weit) verbreitet
common sense	gesunder Menschenverstand
community	Gemeinde, Gemeinschaft
companion	Begleiter(in)
competition	Wettbewerb
concerned	besorgt
confess *v*	gestehen; beichten
confirmation	Bestätigung
confirmed bachelor	überzeugter Junggeselle
confused	verwirrt
conscience	Gewissen
constable	Polizist, Wachtmeister
contract	Vertrag
counter	Tresen, Theke
cove	Bucht
cover *v*	(ab)decken, bedecken
crawl *v*	kriechen, krabbeln

creak *v*	knarren; quietschen
creep, crept, crept *v*	schleichen
cremate *v*	einäschern
crime scene	Tatort
criminal record	Vorstrafe; Vorstrafenregister
cross *v* **one's fingers** *fig*	die Daumen drücken *fig*
crumb	Brösel
curse *v*	fluchen
damn *fam*	verdammt, verflucht *fam*
dare *v* **(to)**	(etwas) wagen
dazed	benommen
dead end	Sackgasse
deadliness	Tödlichkeit
death certificate	Sterbeurkunde
dehydrate *v*	austrocknen, Wasser entziehen
demand	Forderung
demanding	fordernd, anspruchsvoll
dial *v*	wählen (Telefon)
dickie bow	Fliege (Krawatte)
digestion	Verdauung
direction	Richtung
directory enquiries	Telefonauskunft
dirty look	böser Blick
disguise *v*	verstellen, tarnen
disgust	Ekel
dissolve *v*	(sich) auflösen, verflüssigen
distract *v*	ablenken
disturb *v*	stören
dizzy	schwindlig
docks *pl*	Hafen(anlage)
Don't mention it!	Keine Ursache! Nicht der Rede wert!
Dorset	Grafschaft in Südengland
dose	Dosis
do (did, done) *v* **someone a favour**	jemandem einen Gefallen tun
drawer	Schublade
drugged	betäubt
drug-runner	Drogenschmuggler
drug squad	Drogenfahndung

duty sergeant	diensthabender Polizist
easy pickings *pl, fig*	leichte Beute
Egyptian mummy	ägyptische Mumie
elderly	ältere(r), ältlich
emergency service	Notdienst
engaged	verlobt; besetzt
engine	Motor; Maschine
enormous	riesig, enorm
entrance	Eingang, Zugang
envelope	Briefumschlag
equipment	Ausrüstung
escort	Eskorte, Geleitschutz
estate car	Kombiwagen
evidence	Beweis(e)
exclaim *v*	(aus)rufen
expression (on a face)	(Gesichts-)Ausdruck
fair enough	in Ordnung; na schön!
fancy *v* **someone** *fam*	auf jemanden stehen *fam*
file	Akte
fire *v* **someone** *fam*	jemanden feuern *fam*
firmly	fest, hart
flash *v*	(auf)blinken, blitzen
float *v*	treiben, schwimmen
follow *v* **(something) up**	(etwas) weiterverfolgen
for a change	zur Abwechslung
for dear life	um des nackten Lebens willen
forehead	Stirn
fortune	Vermögen
frown *v*	die Stirn runzeln
frustration	Frust, Frustration
fumble *v*	herumtasten
gadget	Gerät, technische Spielerei
gasp *v*	keuchen
general practitioner	Allgemeinmediziner, Hausarzt
gently	sanft
get (got, got) *v* **caught up in**	in etwas verwickelt werden
get (got, got) *v* **on (with someone)**	(mit jemandem) auskommen
get (got, got) *v* **one's skates on** *fig*	ein bisschen dalli machen *fam*

get (got, got) *v* **one's teeth into something** *fig*	sich in etwas hineinknien *fig*
get (got, got) *v* **(straight) down to business** *fig*	(gleich) zur Sache kommen *fig*
get (got, got) *v* **(straight) to the point** *fig*	(gleich) auf den Punkt kommen *fig*
glance *v*	einen Blick werfen (auf)
glove compartment	Handschuhfach
gossip	Tratsch, Klatsch
grab *v*	(zu)packen, schnappen
graveyard	Friedhof
greasy	fettig
greedy	gierig
grim(ly)	grimmig, streng
grimace *v*	das Gesicht verziehen
grin *v*	grinsen
groan *v*	stöhnen
growl *v*	knurren, brummen
grunt *v*	hier: brummeln; grunzen
guide *v*	führen
gut feeling *fam*	Bauchgefühl
halyard	Leine zum Segelsetzen, Fall
handcuffs *pl*	Handschellen
handle	Griff; (Tür-)Klinke
handrail	Handlauf
harden *v*	(sich) (ver)härten, hart werden
hatred	Hass
headquarters	Zentrale, Hauptquartier
headscarf	Kopftuch
hesitate *v*	zögern
hiker	Wanderer/Wanderin
hit	Treffer; Erfolg; Hit
honk *v*	hupen
horse breeder	Pferdezüchter(in)
horseshoe-shaped	hufeisenförmig
housekeeper	Haushälterin
How dare you!	Wie können Sie es wagen!
hug *v*	umarmen
hull	Rumpf (Schiff, Flugzeug)

humour *v* **someone**	jemandem seinen Willen lassen
hunch	(Vor-)Ahnung, Intuition
identity card	Ausweis
I'm afraid (not)	leider (nicht)
imaginary	imaginär, eingebildet
in charge (of)	verantwortlich (für); leiten
in defeat	hier: niedergeschlagen; besiegt
ingredient	Zutat; Bestandteil
insider trading	Insiderhandel (mit Aktien)
insist *v*	beharren, bestehen (auf)
insurance	Versicherung
intently	intensiv, durchdringend
interrogate *v*	verhören, befragen
investigation	Untersuchung, Ermittlung
investigator	Ermittler(in)
irritably	gereizt
jealous (of)	eifersüchtig (auf)
jerk *v*	zucken
the joke is on me *fam*	ich bin der Dumme *fam*
just in case	nur für den Fall, dass ...
kind (of)	Art (von); Sorte (von)
kitchenette	Kochnische
late shift	Spätschicht
latest	hier: neuste(r, s); späteste(r, s); letzte(r, s)
lean, leant, leant *v*	(sich) (an)lehnen; (sich) stützen
lend, lent, lent *v*	(ver)leihen, borgen
let me handle this	lass mich das in die Hand nehmen
let (let, let) *v* **someone down**	jemanden im Stich lassen
lose (lost, lost) *v* **it** *fam*	die Beherrschung verlieren
lounge	Wohnzimmer; Gesellschaftsraum
madness	Wahnsinn
magistrate	Amtsrichter(in)
make	Marke, Fabrikat
malpractice	Berufsvergehen; Amtsmissbrauch
manners *pl*	Manieren, Benehmen
marina	Jachthafen
maritime	See..., maritim
match *v*	passen zu; vergleichen
matter	Sache, Angelegenheit

mayor	Bürgermeister(in)
meanwhile	inzwischen, unterdessen
medical studies	Medizinstudium
menacing	bedrohlich
mercy	Erbarmen, Gnade
mess *v* **someone about**	jemanden an der Nase herumführen
middle-aged	mittleren Alters
minx	freches Ding, Zicke *fam*
mist *v* **up**	(sich) beschlagen
mood	Stimmung, Laune
morgue	Leichenschauhaus
mounted on	montiert auf
mumble *v*	undeutlich sprechen, nuscheln
mutter *v*	(vor sich hin)murmeln, brummeln
nameplate	Namensschild
napkin	Serviette
nasty	scheußlich; böse; gehässig
neat	ordentlich; treffend
nephew	Neffe
newsagent	Zeitungshändler, Zeitschriftenladen
nod *v*	nicken
no matches	keine Treffer
nothing ... but	nichts als, nur
nowadays	heutzutage
objection	Einwand, Einspruch
observe *v*	feststellen, bemerken
obsessed	besessen
obvious(ly)	offensichtlich
Oh dear!	Meine Güte!; Ach du liebe Zeit!
old-fashioned	altmodisch
old maid	alte Jungfer
out of the blue *fig*	unerwartet, aus heiterem Himmel *fig*
overhear, overheard, overheard *v*	zufällig (mit)hören
pat *v*	hier: (Haare) zurechtstreichen; tätscheln
pathologist	Gerichtsmediziner(in)
payment	(Be-)Zahlung

pedestrian	Fußgänger(in)
piano wire	Klavierdraht
pick *v* **clean**	hier: ausplündern
pigsty	Saustall *fam*
pile	Haufen
pinch *v*	zwicken
pin-striped suit	Nadelstreifenanzug
piracy	Piraterie
plump	mollig
poison	Gift
post-mortem (examination)	Obduktion
pour *v*	(ein)gießen, einschenken
prayer	Gebet
presence	Gegenwart, Anwesenheit
press archive	Pressearchiv
presume *v*	vermuten, annehmen
pretend *v*	vorgeben, vortäuschen
proof	Beweis(e)
proper	ordentlich; passend
property	hier: Immobilien; Eigentum, Besitz
proud	stolz
put (put, put) *v* **(someone) through**	(jemanden) durchstellen, verbinden (Telefon)
puzzled	verblüfft, verwirrt
quay	Kai
rage	Wutanfall; Zorn
raise *v*	großziehen; (an)heben
ransom	Lösegeld
rearview mirror	Rückspiegel
receive *v*	erhalten; empfangen
receiver	hier: Hörer; Empfänger
recognition signal	Erkennungszeichen
registration number	polizeiliches Kennzeichen
release *v*	freigeben, freilassen
relive *v* **something**	etwas im Geiste noch einmal erleben
remains *pl*	Überreste
remind *v* **somebody (of something)**	jemanden (an etwas) erinnern

report *v*	melden, berichten; anzeigen
research	Recherche; Forschung
revenge	Rache
rewind button	Rückspultaste
rifle	Gewehr
rigor mortis	Leichenstarre
rocket	Rakete
rope	Seil, Tau
safe house	sicherer Unterschlupf
safety belt	Sicherheitsgurt
save *v* **one's own skin** *fig*	seine eigene Haut retten *fig*
savings *pl*	Ersparnisse
scared (of)	verängstigt, Angst haben (vor)
scowl *v*	ein böses Gesicht machen
scratch *v*	kratzen
scream	Schrei
screech	Quietschen, Kreischen
search warrant	Durchsuchungsbefehl
self-important	selbstgefällig
sense *v*	spüren, fühlen
Serves them right!	Das geschieht ihnen recht!
set (set, set) *v* **off**	sich auf den Weg machen
settle *v* **something**	etwas regeln
severe	heftig; ernst; streng
shame	Schande; Scham
shiver	Zittern
show *v* **someone in(to)**	jemanden hereinführen
shrug *v* **(one's shoulders)**	die Achseln zucken
shuffle *v* **one's feet**	mit den Füßen scharren, schlurfen
sight	Anblick; Sicht; Augen *fig*
signature	Unterschrift
sink, sank, sunk *v*	untergehen; versenken
sip *v*	nippen an; schlürfen
skid *v*	schleudern, rutschen
slave	Sklave/Sklavin
sneer *v*	spöttisch lächeln; höhnen
sniff *v*	schniefen
snore *v*	schnarchen
snort *v*	schnauben, prusten

solve *v*	lösen; aufklären
soul	Seele
spare key	Ersatzschlüssel
special force	Spezialeinheit
speed trap	Radarfalle
spine	Rückgrat; Rücken (Buch)
spinster	Jungfer
squeeze *v*	drücken
St Peter's gates *fig*	Himmel
staircase	Treppe; Treppenhaus
stare *v*	starren
starve *v*	(ver)hungern
state *v*	nennen, angeben; feststellen
steering wheel	Lenkrad
sticky	klebrig
stir *v* **(something)**	(etwas) (um)rühren
stitch	Stich; nähen (Wunde)
stockbroker	Aktienhändler, Börsenmakler
storeroom	Lagerraum
stranded	gestrandet
strangled	erwürgt
stream	Bach
strength	Kraft, Stärke
stroke *v*	streicheln
stud	(Ohr-)Stecker
stunned	benommen; fassungslos
stupidity	Dummheit
sudden	plötzlich; unerwartet
sulk *v*	schmollen
superior	hier: Vorgesetzte(r); besser; überlegen
support *v*	(unter)stützen
suppose *v*	vermuten, annehmen
surgery	hier: Arztpraxis; Chirurgie
suspected	mutmaßlich; tatverdächtig
suspicion	Verdacht
suspicious(ly)	misstrauisch; verdächtig
swallow *v*	(herunter)schlucken
swerve *v*	ausweichen
switch	Schalter

take (took, taken) *v* **advantage of**	ausnutzen
take (took, taken) *v* **aim**	zielen
take (took, taken) *v* **care of**	aufpassen auf, sich kümmern um
take (took, taken) *v* **over**	übernehmen, ablösen
tap	Wasserhahn
tax office	Finanzamt
tea towel	Geschirrtuch
tense	(an)gespannt
That's all for now.	Das war's fürs Erste.
the night before last	vorgestern Abend
theft	Diebstahl
There is more to it than meets the eye.	Da steckt mehr dahinter.
thoughtful(ly)	rücksichtsvoll; nachdenklich
threaten *v*	(be)drohen
tidy	ordentlich, aufgeräumt
tie (tied, tied) *v* **up loose ends** *fig*	Unerledigtes erledigen
tissue	Papiertaschentuch
trace *v*	aufspüren; zurückverfolgen
transfer *v* **(money)**	(Geld) überweisen; verlegen
trapdoor	Falltür
tray	Tablett
trouble-maker	Unruhestifter(in)
trust *v*	(ver)trauen
trusting	vertrauensvoll
tug *v*	zupfen
tut *v*	sich mokieren
tweed	Wollstoff, Tweed
twitch	Zucken, Zuckung
unbearable	unerträglich
unconscious	bewusstlos; unbewusst
understandable	verständlich
undertaker	Bestatter(in)
uneducated	ungebildet
upset	aufgeregt, verärgert
used to	üblicherweise getan haben, gewesen sein
victim	Opfer
villager	Dorfbewohner(in)

wallet	Brieftasche
wallpaper	Tapete
wardrobe	Kleiderschrank
wash *v* **one's dirty linen in public** *fig*	seine schmutzige Wäsche in der Öffentlichkeit waschen *fig*
waste *v*	verschwenden, vergeuden
waste of time	Zeitverschwendung
wave *v* **(one's hands)**	winken
waypoint	Wegpunkt
wedding anniversary	Hochzeitstag
weird	seltsam; unheimlich
whine	Gejammer
whipping	schlagend, peitschend
whisper *v*	flüstern
whistle *v*	pfeifen
will	hier: Testament; Wille
winding	(sich) biegend, windend
wink *v*	zwinkern
wipe *v*	(ab)wischen, (ab)reiben
wipe *v* **out**	auslöschen
witness	Zeuge/Zeugin
wrapper (of sweets)	(Bonbon-)Papier; Verpackung
wrinkle	Falte, Fältchen
yard	Längenmaß: 91 cm; Innenhof
zebra crossing	Zebrastreifen